MW01059852

What seminar attendees are saying about Cyndy Salzmann:

"Now I know that I'm not the only one who sweeps things into a laundry basket to hide in the closet."

"Practical information presented in a humorous way."

"Easy and practical solutions from someone who's been there!"

"Common sense solutions. Cyndy really connects with her audience."

"Inspiring!"

"I now have the urge to rent a garbage truck, back it up to my house and get busy!"

"Cyndy's enthusiasm and love for the Lord is contagious!"

"Cyndy, have you been looking in my cupboards?"

"Much more practical than I expected. I'm actually going to try some of Cyndy's ideas!"

MAKING YOUR HOME A HAVEN

Making Your Home a Haven

Strategies for the Domestically Challenged

Cyndy Salzmann

CHRISTIAN PUBLICATIONS, INC.
CAMP HILL, PENNSYLVANIA

✠ CHRISTIAN PUBLICATIONS, INC.

3825 Hartzdale Drive, Camp Hill, PA 17011
www.christianpublications.com

Making Your Home a Haven
ISBN: 0-88965-206-6
LOC Control Number: 2001-130455
© 2001 by Christian Publications, Inc.
All rights reserved
Printed in the United States of America

03   04   05   06   07   7   6   5   4

Dedication

To John
for your strength, love and encouragement
To Mom
for teaching me to laugh
and most of all
To My Heavenly Father
for drawing me to You and never letting go.

Contents

Foreword

How refreshing it is to read a book about home management that actually makes caring for our homes and families not only sound fun, but also holy! In this excellent primer, Cyndy leads us step-by-step away from chaos to contentment in the home by inviting God into this aspect of everyday living.

What makes this book stand out from other books on home organization and time management is that it first and foremost draws readers from reliance on their own efforts or ingenuity and points them to the source of all practical wisdom and strength—God Almighty. Cyndy wisely offers the reader encouragement and practical suggestions to become proficient in a seldom-mentioned aspect of keeping house—keeping a daily quiet time with the Lord.

Having shown us that the true heart of a home is first establishing a firm foundation with God, this book takes us on a journey through everyday life, which offers practical solutions for everything from getting dinner on the table to digging out from the clutter that threatens to overtake us. (This is a woman who understands us—and our tendency to gather and save. As a reformed gatherer herself, she even admits to collecting sacks of dryer lint once.)

Cyndy has been a dear friend of mine for years. I have been invited to gracious tea parties in her home where, although I was the only guest, she created a cozy afternoon that the Queen of England would have enjoyed.

The atmosphere is one of peace and joy—truly a haven for family and friends.

I have also known Cyndy as a teacher, committed to instructing women in the art of home management from a biblical perspective. I've personally had the pleasure of attending one of the workshops to learn her "Occasional Cooking" method. To watch her orchestrate through mountains of ingredients to quickly produce meal after meal for the freezer was a sight to behold—and the meals we brought home a delight to our husbands!

I cannot recommend this book highly enough. It gives hope and encouragement to the weary, not to mention teaching women how to embrace our roles as homemakers with joy. Bravo Cyndy! And thank you!

Nancy Cobb, Director of Women's Ministries
Christ Community Church
Omaha, Nebraska

INTRODUCTION

Surviving without Alice

A wife of noble character who can find?
She is worth far more than rubies. . . .
She watches over the affairs of her
household
and does not eat the bread of idleness.
Her children arise and call her blessed;
her husband also, and he praises her:
"Many women do noble things,
but you surpass them all."

(Proverbs 31:10, 27-29)

Introduction: Surviving without Alice

It took me a long time to appreciate the Proverbs 31 woman. Growing up, I thought, *Home management? What's to manage?* I blame this attitude on being part of the baby-boom generation who grew up with a steady diet of a marvelous new invention called the television. I remember rushing home after school each day to watch reruns of "Leave It to Beaver" and "Gilligan's Island." After dinner, I'd rush through my homework so I wouldn't miss a second of prime-time favorites like "Charlie's Angels," "The Mary Tyler Moore Show" and "The Brady Bunch." And, like it or not, these shows had a profound impact on me.

Remember "black-and-white" June Cleaver? Mrs. Cleaver made everything look so easy—she even cleaned the bathroom wearing pearls. I thought, *What could be so hard about running a home if you don't even have to take off your pearls?* Things also looked pretty cozy on Gilligan's Island—and Mary Ann didn't even have modern appliances! After living on a deserted island for a few years, I bet Mary Ann wasn't impressed with the Proverbs 31 woman either.

Prime-time shows also made quite an impression on my young mind. I spent considerable time during my high school years trying to mimic Farrah Fawcett's hairstyle. Unfortunately, our humid St. Louis summers frustrated my efforts to create the "big hair" I craved. Consequently, I cut my hair the day after high school graduation and moved on to college to earn a degree in journalism with the intention of working in a newsroom like Mary Tyler Moore. I even set up a cute apartment with a "C" on the wall like Mary's "M." I couldn't wait to toss my beret in the air!

There was only one wrinkle in this wonderful plan for my life . . . Mary, with her exciting career, didn't seem to have a lot of time to bake cookies, arrange flowers and have dinner on the table by 6 o'clock like my black-and-white role model, June Cleaver. I found the solution to my problem with the premier of "The Brady Bunch." Alice did a fine job of taking care of the bothersome details (cleaning, cooking, getting the skunk smell off the dog, etc.) of running a household for Mrs. Brady.

After college, I found a job as a news reporter, moved into my own apartment and quickly met the man of my dreams and future husband. (One up on Mary!) It was beret-tossing time! My new fiancé raved about my culinary skills when he came for dinner, and my two-room apartment with a love seat and an end table was a cinch to keep up. Life was under control—my control.

Happily Ever After

On November 27, 1981, I married the man of my dreams, John Salzmann. Although I still love John with all my heart, it only took about forty-eight hours of wedded bliss for a bit of my own "prime time" reality to creep in. I began to notice that managing a home with a husband wasn't quite as easy as living alone. There were twice as many dishes to wash, double loads of laundry to fold and a toilet seat I was loathe to touch. It was a bit more difficult to have a career like Mary while maintaining my home like June (who strongly resembled my new mother-in-law).

Ever the adoring husband, John enthusiastically offered to divide up household chores. We even made a chore wheel and posted it on the refrigerator. The plan was that one week he would take out the trash and mop the kitchen floor while I did the dishes and cleaned the bathroom. On Saturday, we would turn the wheel and switch jobs. (Isn't that just too sweet for words?) Unfortunately, my husband's idea of cleaning the bathroom made me fear a raid by the health department. And my "constructive" criticism only made matters worse.

> It's better to live on a corner of the roof, than with a
> quarrelsome and ill-tempered wife. (Proverbs 21:9,
> author paraphrase)

Before John actually moved to the roof, God began to help me understand through His Word that my role was to be a "helper" to my husband, who was responsible for leading and providing for our household. One of the passages that hit me right between the eyes is found in the book of Titus.

> Train the younger women to love their husbands and
> children, to be self-controlled and pure, to be busy at
> home, to be kind, and to be subject to their husbands, so
> that no one will malign the word of God. (Titus 2:4-5)

I realized that all of this training in the proper way to clean the toilet and fold laundry wasn't exactly helping him in his role as provider or fulfilling my God-given responsibility to help and support him, in part by creating and maintaining a comfortable home in which we could relax. My heart slowly softened, and I began to see an opportunity in the role God had given me. I began to think, *I can glorify God through the way I manage the house! Cool!* I even reread Proverbs 31.

> *She gets up while it is still dark;*
> *she provides food for her family*
> *and portions for her servant girls.*
> *She considers a field and buys it;*
> *out of her earnings she plants a vineyard.*
> *She sets about her work vigorously;*
> *her arms are strong for her tasks.*
> *She sees that her trading is profitable,*
> *and her lamp does not go out at night.*
> (Proverbs 31:15-18)

As an eternally optimistic baby boomer, I set out to show up the Proverbs 31 woman. I attacked this opportunity with such zeal that my husband wouldn't have been surprised to find me cooking pancakes before sunrise and looking around for investment property! (Remember the old perfume ad, "I can bring home the bacon, fry it up in a pan. . . ." Maybe you don't remember the ad, but if you do, that was me!)

Children

> *Sons are a heritage from the LORD,*
> *children a reward from him.*
> *Like arrows in the hands of a warrior*
> *are sons born in one's youth.*
> *Blessed is the man*
> *whose quiver is full of them.* (Psalm 127:3-5)

In eighteen months our quiver went from zero to three. Each season seemed to bring a surprise. Spring brought our first child, Freddy. In the summer we were appointed legal guardians of my ten-year-old cousin, Donna. And right after Christmas, I found out I was expecting another child. When Liz was born, John and I decided it would be best if I stayed at home with the children while they were young. Although I wholeheartedly agreed with him, I was not about to give up my career. (What would Mary think?) Consequently, I decided to work from home as a public relations consultant—on the kitchen table to be exact. (I am woman! Hear me roar!)

As hard as I tried to keep roaring, before I knew it, our household consisted of a preteen, toddler, newborn, bewildered husband—and a wife/mother/PR consultant who was finally ready to admit she was no match for the woman in Proverbs 31. I needed help! I had finally awakened from my sitcom stupor to the realization that Alice was not a line-item in our family budget.

Chaos

God continued to fill our quiver with the birth of Anna in 1992. And I muddled along trying to juggle my home as well as my home-based business. Each day I waded through piles of laundry, stacks of papers, inches of dust and a mountain of frustration. We ate at fast-food places so often that my children complained they were getting duplicates of the toys in the kids' meals. My husband no longer looked in his drawer for underwear—he went straight to the dryer and let out a war whoop of delight if he found a clean pair. And, even though I had housecleaning help two times a month, I still managed to have the stickiest kitchen floor in Nebraska—perhaps even the free world!

The more I tried to get a handle on the management of my home (even buying a personal library of organization and time-management books), the worse things seemed to get. I finally had to face the truth: I was overcommitted and by all indications severely domestically challenged.

An even more painful admission was the fact that the chaos in our home prevented it from being the haven God intended. The Bible tells us that as followers of Christ, we are strangers in this world (1 Peter 1:1), and we can expect persecution (John 15:20). This is why I so firmly believe our homes need to be a haven from the pressures of the world. A home should be a place where families can feel safe and reconnect and recharge. Unfortunately, the harder I tried to make my home a haven for my family, the deeper I sank into the chaos until I ended up right where I needed to be—on my knees.

View from the Bottom

It was on my knees that I confessed my pride and admitted my failures to God. It was here that Almighty God pried me from my sticky kitchen floor and began to teach me His ways. The first step was to put down my organization books and open the Book that would really help me, the Bible.

> By wisdom a house is built,
>   and through understanding it is established;
> through knowledge its rooms are filled
>   with rare and beautiful treasures. (Proverbs 24:3-4)

To be perfectly honest with you, the wisdom, understanding and knowledge God began to reveal was not easy to take. Just as I had once turned my life over to Him, trust-

ing Him alone for my salvation, He showed me that I
needed to do the same thing with my home. God began to
teach me that it wasn't a clever idea or system that would
turn our home into a haven; it was His work, through me,
that would make a true and lasting difference. He revealed
that I had been depending on myself (and my library of organization books) to manage my home when what I really I
needed was Him.

> *Come to me, all you who are weary and burdened,*
> *and I will give you rest. Take my yoke upon you and*
> *learn from me, for I am gentle and humble in heart, and*
> *you will find rest for your souls. For my yoke is easy and*
> *my burden is light.* (Matthew 11:28-30)

As I cried out to God, He didn't answer with chastise-
ment for bothering Him with such trivial matters as sticky
floors and dirty laundry. Instead, He answered with open
arms, just as He did on the cross when He took the punishment for my sin.

> *Behold! God is mighty, and yet despises no one, nor re-*
> *gards anything as trivial; He is mighty in power of un-*
> *derstanding and heart.* (Job 36:5, AMP)

Like a White Tornado!

He *is* mighty! As I let go, God began to reveal His personal interest in all areas of my life, including the management of my home. And through this intimate
relationship, He has guided me to wise people, helpful
resources and a great janitorial supply store! God even
gave me the confidence to uncover my own talent for organizing and developing systems to help my home run

smoothly. As I changed my focus from me to Him, my home improved dramatically.

Now, I need to pause right here and make sure you understand that my home is far from perfect—and I am quite certain you will never find me cleaning the bathroom in pearls. But I do feel like I generally use my time wisely, spending it on things that are truly important. For example, most nights I can carve out time to have dinner as a family even when John has a meeting, Freddy has a basketball game, Liz has soccer practice and Anna has a riding lesson. I have time for outside activities without feeling overwhelmed, like teaching Bible study and helping in my children's classroom. I often take time to share a cup of tea with a friend or lunch with my husband. And most days I can even find both of my shoes *and* the car keys!

So, why are *you* reading this book? Maybe you're sinking in the mess of your home just as I was. (Maybe you can't find your car keys either. . . .) My prayer is that you, too, will sink all the way to your knees and find that God is there, ready to meet your deepest need. Take it from a mom in the trenches: with Him, I've learned that I *can* survive (and thrive) without Alice!

> *I can do everything through him who gives me strength.*
> (Philippians 4:13)

Going Deeper

1. Who or what influenced your expectations of how to manage a home (e.g., parents, television, friends,

spouse, etc.)? What impact have these influences had on the way you manage your home today?

2. What unexpected challenges did you face in the area of home management when you moved from your parents' home into your first home or apartment? What new challenges occurred over the years, and how did they affect you? What challenges are you facing now?

3. Read Genesis 2:18. Use a dictionary to discover what it means to be a "suitable helper" to your husband. How does this relate to the management of our homes?

4. Read Proverbs 31:10-31. Describe the character and list the activities of this "superwoman." From where does she draw her strength? (See 31:30.) What does God expect from a "wife of noble character" today? (See Titus 2:3-5.)

5. Read Matthew 11:28-30. What is God saying to you personally in this verse? How do we practically accept Jesus' invitation when it comes to the management of our homes?

6. In the Amplified Bible, Job 36:5 says, "Behold! God is mighty, and yet despises no one, nor regards *anything as trivial*; He is mighty in power of *understanding and heart*" (emphasis added). List the attributes of God described in this verse. What comfort and hope do you draw from this passage? How does this apply to managing your home?

7. How would you define the word "haven"? Does this word describe your home? If not, what do you think is standing in the way?

8. Take a few minutes to visualize your home as a haven. What do you see? Share this vision with the group.

9. How can your home, as a haven, minister to you? To your family? To others?

10. Think about the areas of managing your home that are the most difficult for you. Then, spend some time in prayer. During this time, turn over each of these difficult areas—one by one—to God. Tell Him of your desire for your home to be a haven for your family and others. Ask Him to make changes—in His way and in His time.

CHAPTER ONE

Finding a Quiet Place

Come, let us go up to the mountain of
the LORD,
to the house of the God of Jacob.
He will teach us his ways,
so that we may walk in his paths.
(Isaiah 2:3)

Finding a Quiet Place

I know what you're thinking. You're tempted to skip this chapter and move on to the parts of the book which help you organize your closets and the mountain of paper that has taken over your counters. You may have a desire to deepen your relationship with God, but you need to get things at home under control first. There is no way you can add one more thing to your schedule. You are barely keeping your head above water right now. . . . If you don't do something quickly . . .

I understand. I truly understand because I've been there. I have been right where you are. I need to tell you that your plan will *not* work. I had to learn the hard way that the key is not finding a great system or method which works for you—it's finding God and putting Him first in all things. If you go to God first, He will fill you, help you and stretch your time. I don't know how He does it. I only know that He is Almighty God—and He does! "Seek first his kingdom and his righteousness, and all these things will be given to you as well" (Matthew 6:33).

The power behind any ministry is taking the time to seek God's will through prayer and reading the Bible. Your ministry in the home is no different. The purpose of seeking God is not to give you standards to meet, but to bring you to the One who will and can help.

> If you completely give of yourself physically, you become exhausted. But when you give of yourself spiritually, you get more strength.

> —Oswald Chambers
> *My Utmost for His Highest*, August 2

It didn't take much for God to convince me I needed strength—and there was no question I was exhausted. I was sinking fast and Jesus' words struck a chord in the very pit of my soul:

> *I am the vine; you are the branches. If a man remains in me and I in him, he will bear much fruit; apart from me you can do nothing.* (John 15:5)

Well, I definitely wasn't bearing fruit anyone would consider eating, and my heart was crying out for nourishment. I knew the best way to stay connected to the Vine was through a daily quiet time of prayer and Bible reading. But, with four children at home, that was easier said than done. Time alone, much less quiet time alone, was something I hadn't experienced in several years. But, ever the optimistic baby boomer . . .

Finding Time with God

> *When you pray, go into your room, and when you have shut your door, pray to your Father who is in the secret place; and your Father who sees in secret will reward you openly.* (Matthew 6:6, NKJV)

My first attempt at trying to establish a regular quiet time came shortly after convincing my husband we needed a wing chair for the bedroom. I explained that I needed a place for my quiet time where I could shut the door and block out the chaos waiting just outside of it.

A few days after the chair was in place, I sat my children down and explained I needed some time alone with God. With my oldest in charge and a movie in the VCR, I went into the bedroom and shut the door. Although a closed door is irresistible to small children, my real mistake was telling them I wanted some "time alone with God." The kids couldn't resist an opportunity to see God talking to Mommy in her bedroom! I had barely reached my new wing chair when I saw noses peeking under the door.

Patiently, I clarified my request. I explained that God was with me, but invisible. What I needed was a quiet place to pray and read the Bible—alone. This time, determined to have at least ten minutes to pray, I locked the door. I'm sure all of you mothers can guess what happened next. Before I knew it, notes were being slipped under the door with all sorts of "emergencies."

Plan B was to pray early in the morning before the children woke up. I soon became convinced that children are wired with an alarm that wakes them as soon as their mother's big toe touches the floor. Before I even opened my Bible, I would invariably hear, "Mommy, I need you! Did you know we're all out of Fruit Loops?" To be in such demand . . .

Frustration mounting, I moved on to Plan C. I had recently read a book which recounted a story about the mother of John Wesley. She had many children (at least nine!). She would pull her apron over her head as a signal to the family that she was praying and was not to be disturbed. At this point, I had nothing to lose and reasoned I might even make a memory for my children as well as carve out time for prayer.

First, I dug an apron out and began to put it on. That action in itself attracted a considerable amount of attention from my children. I could just see their little minds churning, *What in the world is Mommy doing now?* Nevertheless, I explained, "Whenever you see an apron over my head, like this (demonstrating), I am talking to God. So don't disturb me, OK?" With the ground rules clear, I sat down at the kitchen table, pulled the apron over my head and tried to calm myself enough to begin praying.

To be honest, I felt a little silly under the apron (OK, extremely silly), but thought I would eventually get used to my new "prayer closet." It wasn't until I heard a small giggle, then uncontrollable laughter, that I realized I had definitely succeeded in creating a memory—but not a prayer time.

Still not ready to give up, I decided to try praying at night when the kids were already asleep. I tried to use the ACTS (Adoration, Confession, Thanksgiving, Supplication) formula to keep me focused, but I almost always fell asleep before I even reached "T." I tried kneeling by my bed, but spots on the carpet or dust bunnies behind the dresser always distracted me.

It seemed no matter how hard I tried to pray, I could not keep my focus. I would be praying for my daughter and remember that her book order was due the next day. Or I would be praying for my husband and start thinking about how I wished he wouldn't leave his shirts hanging on the bedpost. There always seemed to be something to distract or interrupt me!

Prayer was the most frustrating part of my walk with God . . . my silent walk with God. I could send up arrow prayers or fall to my knees when I was upset. I could pray in groups or with friends. But consistent one-on-one communication with God just wasn't happening.

Changes for Cyndy

As I look back, I wonder how I got along. . . . How can you be close to someone to whom you talk only superficially? I spent a lot of time listening to other people talk about God, but very little time talking to Him, or more importantly, coming to the place where I could hear His whispers in my heart.

So what changed? Something really quite simple. I began to journal . . . to write my prayers out instead of speaking them. My journal began as letters *to* God which quickly evolved into conversations *with* God.

The changes in my life began when a friend invited me to a workshop on prayer at her church. I was not exactly excited, but had heard the speaker was funny and had a powerful testimony. Not far into the workshop, the speaker shared that she has prayed for an hour each day for the last fifteen years. My mouth literally fell open. I nudged my friend and said, "I don't believe it! This woman taught aerobics classes, for goodness sake!"

As the workshop went on, the speaker described how she prays for an hour each day. She writes her prayers in letter form to God in a journal. My ears perked up. When I was younger, I loved to write notes and letters. The idea of baring my soul through a letter to God Almighty appealed to me. Maybe this could work for me.

The next day I pulled out a spare notebook and spent forty-five minutes in prayer, concentrated prayer. I actually had to stop myself. I felt closer to God than I could ever remember. It was like coming home after a long absence. God ministered to me so much during that time, touching me at the deepest part of my soul. I couldn't wait until the next morning.

The next day, I got up early, and of course, so did my children. This time, when I was interrupted, I looked up from my prayer journal, pen still poised on the paper, and calmly said, "Then have Corn Flakes instead of Fruit Loops," and picked up right where I had left off. It was marvelous.

I have found that putting pen to paper slows me down and keeps me focused on the Person I am talking to, God Almighty. Because my prayers are written, I can resume my train of thought if interrupted. I'm not exactly sure why journaling works, why the connection isn't broken by distractions. I just know it works.

Pray without Ceasing

Now I can pray anywhere, and I generally have to stop myself after an hour. I can pray early in the morning, late at night, in my favorite chair, on an airplane or at the neighborhood bagel shop (my personal favorite).

I am a regular at the bagel shop near my home. I order a cup of coffee and a blueberry bagel, sit down and pour my heart out to God for at least an hour. He renews and refreshes me so much during that hour that I literally bounce out of the shop.

Before my youngest daughter, Anna, started school, I would bring her with me to the bagel shop. It was a very special time for us and a memory I will always cherish. She had her own prayer journal in which she would draw pictures praising and thanking God. I would draw little pictures at the top of each page to help guide her through her prayer time. A heart (praise) reminded her to draw a picture of something she loves about God. The next picture had a sad face (confession) to prompt her to draw a picture illustrating something she may have done wrong and for which she was sorry. The next page had a smiling face (thanksgiving), where she could express her thanks to God. And, the last page, had a stick figure of a little girl on her knees (supplication) where she could lay her requests, or petitions, before God.

I still marvel at how quiet and content Anna was during that hour. (It soon dawned on me that she needed a quiet time with God, too.) One morning, another customer at the bagel shop stopped by our table. She said to Anna, "You are such a good girl to color so quietly while your Mom works. Good job, Mom! I'm impressed." She wouldn't have been too impressed if I told her about the apron incident.

Helping my daughter establish the habit of journaling has had a powerful impact on her relationship with God. Let me share an example that still fills my husband and me with awe.

One day after our quiet time at the bagel shop, I asked Anna if she would like to share her journal with me and tell me about her pictures. When she came to the "petition" page, she had drawn a picture of a little girl walking a dog in the rain. She said she asked Jesus for a puppy, and He told her "in her heart" that He would give her one in the spring.

I was stunned—and not just because the last thing I needed was a dog! I was stunned because just the night before, my husband and I discussed (while alone in the car) getting a family dog in the spring because Anna has such a love for animals. We both agreed to keep this a deep secret from the children in case we came to our senses and changed our minds. Little did we know that Almighty God had other plans and was answering the faithful prayer of our daughter. Even more awesome was the realization that Anna's habit of having a quiet time had brought her to the point of being able to hear and discern the voice of God—even before she started kindergarten! I can't wait to see what He has planned for Anna's future.

> *"For I know the plans I have for you"* declares the LORD, *"plans to prosper you and not to harm you, plans to give you hope and a future. Then you will call upon me and come and pray to me, and I will listen to you. You will seek me and find me when you seek me with all your heart."* (Jeremiah 29:11-13)

How to Get Started

Before I share a little bit about the system I use for my quiet time, it's important to remember that what works for me may not work for you. But, while we are all different, we all have the same need for intimacy with God. So I encourage you to go to God and ask Him to help you find a way to set aside some quality time with Him each day. God will show you how and where He wants you to meet Him—and you may be surprised by His answer.

Whether you decide to try journaling or not, the first thing you need to do is make a decision to begin a regular quiet time. I'm talking about a real commitment, not a wishy-washy, good-intentions kind of decision but a firm commitment to God that you will work hard to keep.

Once you have made the decision to begin a quiet time, it's important to decide specifically when and where you will meet God the *next* day. I keep a "prayer rock" on my pillow to remind me to set my quiet time for the next morning. (Instructions for making your own prayer rock are included in the resources section at the back of the book.) I also pray and ask God to help me keep the commitment. Until your quiet time becomes a habit, it's a good idea to write this "appointment" down (perhaps on a sticky note) and stick it somewhere you will be sure to notice.

I like to spend time with God first thing in the morning, if possible. Before my head hits the pillow at night, my prayer rock reminds me to review the next day's schedule in my mind, make an appointment with God and ask Him to help me keep it. I have found that it is very rare when something interferes with the time I have set.

It's also helpful to designate a time and place where you will most often meet God for your quiet time. It could be a comfortable chair, the kitchen table or the back porch—anyplace that is comfortable and inviting. At home, my place is a comfortable chair in the family room. I like this chair because it has a cozy blanket, an ottoman for my feet, and right across the room is a picture of Jesus as a carpenter. It's a reminder that He is working on me each day, smoothing my rough edges. Since I don't want thoughts of housework to interfere with my time with God, I make sure this room is picked up before I go to bed.

You will find it helpful to keep the things you'll need for your quiet time conveniently near the place you have chosen. A basket, chest or box works well to corral such items. The basket next to my chair holds a variety of things, including my prayer journal, Bible, hymnbook and assorted devotionals. I also keep a good supply of pens that I especially like to write with there. I get a certain pleasure from using a pen with ink that just flows over the paper. (I'll resist telling you the brands I like best!)

I keep my prayer journal in my planner which includes a calendar and to-do list. I've found having a to-do list handy keeps my mind from wandering. If I think of something that needs to be added during my prayer time (such as making a phone call or sending a birthday card), I make a quick note, then resume my prayers.

My prayer journal is in a five-by-seven-inch three-ring binder that zips and has extra pockets for prayer guides, sticky notes, spare change, etc. Having the journal in my planner works well for me. You may prefer a pretty book with blank pages, the kind that are sold at most card shops or bookstores. Some devotional books are also designed with space for journaling, or you may choose to use a simple spiral notebook. Plain or fancy, the key is to make it functional and convenient. Your journal should be something that is easy to write in and can easily be taken with you—perhaps to the bagel shop.

Structuring Your Meeting with God

Once I settle in my chair, usually with a cup of coffee or tea nearby, I open my journal and head off to the "mountain of the LORD!" (Isaiah 2:3). Each day is a refreshing new experience.

While structure can be helpful to guide you through the prayer time, don't let ritual quench the leading of the Holy Spirit. For example, some mornings I feel led to begin my quiet time with a song. Other days, I may start out by reading from a devotional. Or, I may dive right into Scripture, perhaps praising God by reading a psalm. My point is to avoid allowing external things to interfere with God's leading.

Now that I've sufficiently warned you about the hazards of structure, I will confess that the time I actually spend in concentrated prayer is generally structured. Specifically, I often find it helpful to use the ACTS formula to guide my prayer time. You will remember that ACTS stands for **A**doration, **C**onfession, **T**hanksgiving and **S**upplication. (You may be familiar with a similar acronym, PRAY, which can stand for **P**raise, **R**epent, **A**sk, **Y**ield.)

Adoration

Praise be to the LORD, my Rock. . . .
He is my loving God and my fortress,
my stronghold and my deliverer,
my shield, in whom I take refuge. (Psalm 144:1-2)

Begin your prayer time by praising God for who He is and what He's done. As mentioned earlier, I often find it helpful to begin by reading a psalm. These beautiful poems recounting God's character and deeds spur me to overflow with praise. I may rewrite a psalm in my journal or reword it as my own hymn of praise to God. You might enjoy constructing your own alphabet of praise by writing down an attribute of God that corresponds to each letter (awesome, benevolent, Creator, etc.). Or you may want to praise God by recounting what He has done in your life or the lives of others. You can find a wonderful example of this in Exodus 15:1-18 in the beautiful song Moses and the Israelites sang to the Lord to thank Him for their rescue from Egypt. Regardless of how you choose to praise God, praise is a wonderful way to open the way into the presence of the Almighty with proper reverence and appreciation.

Confession

Search me, O God, and know my heart;
test me and know my anxious thoughts.
See if there is any offensive way in me,
and lead me in the way everlasting.
(Psalm 139:23-24)

After praising God by recounting His attributes and faithfulness, my own heart looks pretty dirty. God desires us to present ourselves as clean and holy vessels. This is only possible by confession of our sin followed by forgiveness through the sacrifice of Jesus Christ.

Create in me a pure heart, O God,
and renew a steadfast spirit within me.
(51:10)

During this time of confession, humbly ask God to search your heart and reveal your sin. Take your time. Be still. Allow the Holy Spirit to reveal your sins. A note of caution: if you are writing your confession in a journal, the possibility exists for it to be read by another person. If your sin has the potential to hurt someone else, you may want to be discreet. God knows your heart and your desire for forgiveness.

As you confess your sins, allow God's love and forgiveness to wash over you. Put your sins behind you, just as God has cast them "as far as the east is from the west" (103:12).

> Though your sins are like scarlet,
> they shall be as white as snow. (Isaiah 1:18)

Resist the temptation to hold on to your sins, like taking the pieces of a broken teacup from the wastebasket to examine them. We must leave the broken pieces in the trash where they won't cut us or others. The same is true with your sin; don't allow it to stand between you and God. Accept God's forgiveness, and move ahead hand in hand.

> I . . . am he who blots out
> your transgressions, for my own sake,
> and remembers your sins no more. (43:25)

Thanksgiving

> Give thanks to the LORD, call on His name;
> make known among the nations what he has done.
> (Psalm 105:1)

By now, you may find your heart overflowing with the goodness and tenderness of God. Take this opportunity to thank Him for all He has done in your life. Thank Him for His provision for your family and your ministry to others. Thank Him specifically for the many blessings He has showered upon you.

One of my favorite aspects of journaling is that my prayer journal becomes a private record of miracles. During this time, I enjoy reviewing my prayers and petitions from the past few days and thank God specifically for His answers. It is awesome to see how God has worked in so many ways both large and small. It's important that we acknowledge these answers with our heartfelt thanks.

Supplication

I thank and praise you, O God of my fathers . . .
you have made known to me what we asked of you.
(Daniel 2:23)

Ask and you will receive, and your joy will be complete.
(John 16:24)

The last part of ACTS stands for supplication. In other words, this is a time to put your requests or petitions before God. What an awesome honor to be granted access to God Almighty who promises to hear and answer our prayers!

Some people may think because a prayer is being written down in a journal, the request better be something really important. But God tells us to pray about all things.

Do not be anxious about anything, but in everything,
by prayer and petition, with thanksgiving, present your
requests to God. (Philippians 4:6)

In addition to the really big things, I pray about the little things, like being tired, finding time to exercise, remembering to send lunch money, gaining a better attitude about laundry—all sorts of things. And I love to see the creative ways God answers. I just have to share the following example of how God honored a request for one of the little things in my life.

A few years ago, I was on an airplane heading to the fourth city in four days as part of a business trip. As a communication consultant, I had been conducting focus groups and interviews from early in the morning until late in the evening for one of my clients who had locations throughout the country. Later, I would have a long dinner with this woman to discuss the day's findings. She happened to be ten years younger than I—and appeared to need much less sleep.

So, here I was on an airplane, explaining to God in my prayer journal how totally exhausted I was. As I was pleading for strength and renewal, specifically asking Him not to let me fall asleep in the middle of a sentence, my client mentioned that there was only one hotel available in the city to which we were heading, and she hoped it wasn't, in her words, "a flea bag." With this heartwarming possibility, I continued writing in my prayer journal, asking God to "puleez" take care of the hotel arrangements so I could get a good night's sleep—and perhaps a bit of exercise.

As we pulled up to the hotel, I was shocked to see the letters on the marquee proclaiming, "Welcome Cyndy Salzmann! Guest of the Day!" Totally bewildered, I went to the registration desk and said, "Hello. I'm Cyndy Salzmann . . . " and before I could get another word out of my mouth, the clerk put on an electric smile and said, "Oh! Welcome, Ms. Salzmann! You are our Guest of the Day! Here is your gift bag!" He then handed me a sack packed with treats, coffee, snacks, a mug, special tea, soaps—all sorts of goodies—then added, "As Guest of the Day, you have been assigned our Nordic Spa Room!" He explained that it was a special room with upgraded sheets, a down comforter and pillows, purified air and water and—a "Nordic Trac Walk Fit" treadmill in the room. I was floored! Enjoying the amenities of the Nordic Spa Room offered just the excuse I needed to order dinner in and get some rest.

I felt great when I arrived home to see my family the following evening. What a fun God we have! He not only gave me a good night's sleep, but He also made me "Guest of the Day!"

> What makes God so dear to us is not so much His big blessings to us, but the tiny things, because they show us His amazing intimacy with us. He knows every detail of each of our individual lives.
>
> —Oswald Chambers
> *My Utmost for His Highest*, June 3

Take Time to Listen

Do you remember the story of Mary and Martha? Luke 10:38-42 recounts a visit to their home by Jesus. Martha is in the kitchen preparing dinner for her Lord, while her sister, Mary, is sitting at His feet listening to Him teach. Martha complains about doing all the work herself and asks Jesus to tell Mary to get up and help her. Jesus surprises Martha with His reply that Mary has made the right choice to spend time with Him.

"Sure, but who's going to make dinner?" you ask. Before you peg Mary as the lazy younger sister, let's look at this story from her point of view. Perhaps she thought, *This man just fed 5,000 people. I'm not going to worry about dinner (Matthew 14:13-21). He can handle it."* Or maybe she had already asked Jesus if He would like her to make dinner and He said, "Don't worry about it. I want to talk to you first." The point is, she was aware of God's will for her at that moment.

The lesson for us from this story is the importance of taking the time, even with so many things beckoning us, to listen to what God has to say and apply His truth to our lives. We can hear God's voice in many ways—through the Bible, in prayer, in the stillness of the moment—but we have to make the time to do so.

Have you ever read the Bible in its entirety? If not, why not start today? There are even special one year Bibles to help you with this process. This type of Bible is set up with passages from both the Old and New Testaments as well as a psalm and proverb for each day. This was the method I used to read the Bible for the first time.

There are also many devotional books set up to be used on a daily basis. One of my favorites is *My Utmost for His Highest* by Oswald Chambers. There are also devotions specifically designed to offer encouragement to wives and mothers. Check your Christian bookstore, and ask God to direct you to the devotional that will speak directly to your heart.

It's important not to rush this time of listening. As you read through Scripture or a devotional, pause to reflect on what God is saying to you. You just may want to sit quietly and think about a specific passage of Scripture or reflect on God's character or His ways. You might even have some questions for God. There are many examples in the Bible of God's people questioning Him. Hannah, King David and Habakkuk are just a few who poured out their questions and concerns before God. They also took time to listen to His answers.

You may want have a special section of your journal just for listening. That's where I record promptings and lessons from God as well as my questions. Be sure to record the answers to your questions and how they came to you. Perhaps God directed you to a passage in the Bible that answered your question, or spoke to you through another person, or perhaps you heard His voice in the stillness of your soul. These times of listening to God, of sitting at His feet like Mary, are the most precious to me.

Be still, and know that I am God. (Psalm 46:10)

Expect to Change

What I wasn't expecting as a result of a consistent, concentrated quiet time was the dramatic change in my relationship with God. It is hard to even write about this without my eyes filling with tears. And to think, I had gone all these years without realizing the hunger in my soul. I think Job says it best:

I had heard of You [only] by the hearing of the ear; but now my [spiritual] eye sees You. (Job 42:5, AMP)

After just a few weeks of concentrated prayer and seeking, I began to feel so close to God. We were walking together all the time, as if we were fused. Every decision, every act, everything seemed to be filtered through His eyes . . . which were now my eyes. I looked for God in all things—and found Him in everything.

Prayer is not a matter of changing things externally—but one of working miracles in a person's inner nature. Prayer is coming into perfect fellowship and oneness with God.

—Oswald Chambers
My Utmost for His Highest, August 28

So . . .

> before you read another word of this book
> before you open a closet door to clean it
> before you tackle that stack of papers
> . . . make an appointment to meet
>   Almighty God—and keep it!

> *The LORD will guide you always;*
> *he will satisfy your needs in a sun-scorched land*
> *and will strengthen your frame.*
> *You will be like a well-watered garden,*
> *like a spring whose waters never fail.* (Isaiah 58:11)

Going Deeper

1. Share a time when you experienced the power of prayer in your life or another person's life.

2. What obstacles have you faced when trying to establish and keep a regular quiet time with God? What could you do to overcome these obstacles?

3. Read Matthew 6:33. Why should we seek God first? What benefits are derived from our obedience to this command? How can we specifically and practically make this a habit in our everyday lives?

4. Read John 15:5. What is Jesus saying to believers with this verse? How does this apply to our ministry at home?

5. How do we develop intimacy with another person? How do we develop intimacy with God?

6. Have you ever used a journal to pray? If so, would you share your experience? How might journaling facilitate concentrated prayer?

7. Review the ACTS structure for prayer. Have you ever used this or another structure while praying? How might using this or a similar tool help during our prayer times? How might structure hinder our time with God?

8. Read Luke 10:38-42. What interferes with your ability to listen to God? In what ways can we hear God's voice today?

9. If you have established a regular quiet time, would you share what has helped you remain faithful to this commitment? How have you been blessed by your time with God?

10. Read Isaiah 58:11. What encouragement do you receive from this verse?

CHAPTER TWO

Digging Out

For where your treasure is, there your heart will be also. (Matthew 6:21)

Digging Out

There was a time in my life when I actually saved dryer lint (and felt good about it). I also saved used dryer sheets. My intention was to twist the dryer sheet around the lint and use it for a fire starter. For almost a year, I kept a bag of lint and a bag of dryer sheets hanging from a peg in my garage. Pretty incredible, eh?

What's even more incredible is that I didn't come up with this idea myself. I found this "helpful hint" in a magazine article entitled something like "Taking a Second Look at Trash." (Wouldn't it seem I could find a better use of my time than contemplating our trash, like perhaps removing it from the house?) The author of the article also shared a recipe for using dryer lint to make play dough. I hadn't gotten around to trying the recipe or actually making up some fire starters before I realized I had a problem.

I never considered myself a pack rat (and my husband would certainly never call me overly frugal), but I tended to hang on to things—just in case—like, just in case we ran out of play dough, and I needed to make up an emergency batch with my dryer lint.

As my family grew, it began to take a lot of my time to maintain all the things I was collecting. I used to keep single socks and gloves thinking the mates would turn up; or video tapes of programs I had recorded, but never got around to watching. The list goes on and on. . . .

I began to think of all the time I spent collecting and caring for all this stuff in my home, much like painting firewood. It was all going to burn in the end, so why should I get burned out trying to keep it organized and dusted? I finally began to realize that we all have to let go of the temporal (stuff) in order to uncover the spiritual treasure God has for us.

Loosening Your Grip

Their possessions were too great for them to remain together. (Genesis 36:7)

Before implementing any systems in this book for improving the management of your home, you must get rid of the clutter in your life. "What clutter?" you may ask. Ironically, most people who have a lot of clutter in their homes feel the problem is a lack of storage. Take my word for it (as a reformed collector of dryer lint)—the problem is not a lack of storage. If you don't have room to store your stuff, you simply have too much stuff.

I have a friend who keeps a jar of puppy teeth in her kitchen drawer, including the teeth of those pets who have already died. Another friend still has her teenage daughter's umbilical cord. A good friend of mine hangs on to all of her kids' Happy Meal boxes in case they might want to play with them. One friend confided to me that she kept her son's dead parakeet in the freezer for eighteen months, while another woman admitted that her closet held a bag of dirt from her vacuum cleaner for an entire year because she thought it might contain an earring. (It did, but that's not the point!)

All right, maybe you don't have any dead pets in your freezer, puppy teeth in your kitchen drawer or bags of dirt in your closet. But there are many things we all have a tendency to hang on to. Here is a partial list of things you can toss right now:

- pantyhose with runs
- pens that don't work
- earrings without mates
- used foil or ziplock bags
- plastic souvenir cups (no family should have more than six)
- underwear, socks or shoes with holes (What would the emergency room staff think if you were in an accident?)
- socks and gloves without mates
- plastic containers without lids
- plastic lids without containers
- old greeting cards
- expired coupons (or all coupons if you rarely use them)
- children's artwork (other than a few memorable pieces)
- old magazines and newspapers
- broken toys or games with missing pieces
- old travel guides or maps
- coloring books with the pictures colored
- wire hangers

- old paperback books
- soap slivers (sorry, Grandma Clark)
- more than a month's supply of rubber bands or twist ties
- old seeds
- dead batteries
- and most importantly, *clothes that hurt!*

I'm sure you can think of many more things to add to this list. The key to digging out is not to allow yourself to feel overwhelmed by the enormity of the task. Start by cleaning out one small drawer. Just take a deep breath, whisper a prayer, grit your teeth and dig in!

Getting Started

> *There is a time for everything,*
> *and a season for every activity under heaven: . . .*
> *a time to search and a time to give up,*
> *a time to keep and a time to throw away.*
> (Ecclesiastes 3:1, 6)

The starting point in my personal clutter control campaign was the drawer which held my kitchen utensils. It always jammed when I tried to open or close it. When I finally got it open, I couldn't find what I needed.

The first thing to go from this drawer was a tool used to stamp a design in a stick of butter. That was easy to toss—I had yet to decorate my butter in twelve years of marriage and didn't see that changing. Next, I came upon the melon-baller. This was a bit more difficult. I never knew if I would get the urge to make a fancy melon salad. Since I hadn't done so in ten years, I reluctantly threw it out.

I have to admit, it was tricky to determine just how many wooden spoons I needed. I realized eighteen was too many. I took a gulp and settled on my four favorites. The end result was a drawer I could open and actually find the tool I needed. I never knew cooking could be so simple!

The Five R's

I call my personal system of de-junking "The Five Rs of Clutter Control." I like this system because it allows me to clear away the stuff that complicates our lives without leaving the house in a shambles during the process.

Here's how it works. Round up four fairly large containers and a large, heavy-duty trash bag. I like to use boxes or plastic containers with lids. Make five labels: Refuse, Recycle, Remove, Repair and Relocate. You will use these containers (instead of little piles) to help sort your stuff as you move around the house from drawer to drawer and closet to closet.

Refuse

Label the trash bag "Refuse." Use this for all things that should go out with the trash. This will probably be the most full when you finish, so keep a generous supply on hand. It's best if your "Refuse" bag is not of the clear variety. You would hate to have the little pack rats that may live in your home "rescuing" their junk and undoing your hard work.

You may be thinking, *Well, you know Cyndy, one person's trash is another's treasure.* Forgive me for being blunt, but it's been my experience with those who tend to hang on to things think that it's all treasure—or might be someday.

> *Whatever is true, whatever is noble, whatever is right,*
> *whatever is pure, whatever is lovely, whatever is admira-*
> *ble—if anything is excellent or praiseworthy—think*
> *about such things [and toss the rest!].* (Philippians 4:8)

Recycle

> *The LORD God took the man and put him in the Garden*
> *of Eden to work it and take care of it.* (Genesis 2:15)

If you are reading this book, I can just about guarantee that environmental regulations have changed since you last cleaned out your closets, drawers and storage areas. That's why I suggest labeling the next container "Recycle."

There are many things we can't (or shouldn't) send to the local landfill. This container is for the things that can be recycled. Items in this container might include chemicals, old paint and oil, newspapers, magazines or plastic, glass, tin or aluminum containers. Don't let this container sit around for very long. Recycle or properly dispose of the contents promptly. (Remember, keep chemicals, etc., away from young children.)

Just a word of caution. Recycling is good stewardship of the earth God has charged us to care for. But it is important to be realistic and keep some perspective. You don't have to try to find a way to recycle everything, or use this as an excuse to hang on to your stuff. Your home was not meant to substitute as a landfill.

Remove

Label the next container "Remove." This is for things that you don't need but might be useful to someone else.

Do not place things in here that should go into your trash bag. Make sure the individual or organization really wants your empty egg cartons or margarine tubs before you give them to them. If it is junk to you, it is probably junk to someone else. Toss it. (The only exception concerns the possessions of your children. I'll get to this at the end of the chapter.)

Here are some examples of items that might end up in my "Remove" container. About once a year, I remove all the travel-sized shampoo, lotion and soap we've collected from hotels and pass them along to the local homeless shelter. I give leftover wallpaper or craft supplies to my child's classroom. The toys that come in kid's meals are saved for short-term missionaries to hand out on their trips overseas. Old greeting cards go to the women's circle at church who recycle them to raise money for the Good Samaritan Fund. I save only the best of my children's clothing to hand down to relatives or pass along to a women's shelter. I can't tell you how much fun it was to give away my "power suits" to an organization that helps needy women who are entering the workforce!

The key here is to give these things away promptly to an individual or organization that can use them. One good hint is to slip the items you plan to give away into a plastic grocery sack labeled with the intended recipient before even placing them in your "Remove" container. This saves time and makes it much easier to actually remove the items from your home.

Another way to remove items from your home is to have a garage sale and give what doesn't sell to a worthwhile organization. If you have pack-rat tendencies, I strongly recommend not having a garage sale. It's tempting to bring your stuff back in the house after you've spent all day looking at it, and much too tempting for husbands and children. Personally, my advice is to skip the garage sale and give everything in this box away.

If you do decide to have a garage sale, consider having a "name your own price" sale. Here's how it works: Just set your stuff out and tell people who stop by that they can name the price they are willing to pay for items they would like to purchase. Most people will offer a fair price, but for those few who may not, keep in mind that your goal is to remove the things you don't need from your home. (Many people pay others to do just that!)

When I held this type of garage sale, it was the least amount of work, I made the most money and got rid of almost everything I had for sale! An added benefit was selling Anna's snowsuit to a single mom at a bargain price and seeing our used trundle bed go to an immigrant family with triplets.

> *He who gives to the poor will lack nothing,*
> *but he who closes his eyes to them receives many curses.*
> (Proverbs 28:27)

Repair

Pack rats, like myself, have a tendency to keep all sorts of things that can't be used or worn because they are in need of repair. We have good intentions to fix these things, but it never seems to get done. My children would groan when a favorite item of clothing would get a rip or a zipper would break. They knew too well that when I said to put the item in my mending basket that they might as well kiss it good-bye.

To avoid this problem and catch up on those pesky "to do" chores, label another container "Repair," and use it for all of those items that need some attention before they can be useful. I've found that this is a good container to keep around permanently. In addition to prodding you either to repair or remove, you may find that having items in need of repair in a central location will motivate your husband to do a little handyman work. If not, repair the item yourself, hire someone else do the work or throw it away. My rule is to toss anything still in the repair box after thirty days. There is no reason for keeping something you can't use or wear. In our house, good intentions have a thirty-day expiration date!

> *If a man is lazy, the rafters sag;*
> *if his hands are idle, the house leaks.*
> (Ecclesiastes 10:18)

Relocate

Label the final container "Relocate." Place things in this container that should more logically be kept in another place. (For example, why keep a hammer in your bathroom drawer or photos in with the silverware?) When you are cleaning out the area where an item in your "Relocate" container belongs, just put it in its proper place.

When I went through my first dejunking process, one of my goals was to get my collection of cookbooks off the kitchen counter. The books were a pain to move every time I cleaned up the counters, and the spines had become splattered with everything from strained peaches to spaghetti sauce. My problem was finding a new, convenient location for them in my overstuffed home.

The books sat in my "Relocate" container for a couple of weeks while I worked my way around the kitchen (tossing butter molds and souvenir cups) until I reached the pantry. When I had finished cleaning this bastion of clutter, I found that I had an entire shelf open—a perfect place for the cookbooks. Miracles never cease!

As I hope you can see, the key to the success of this process is to be absolutely ruthless. Your goal is not just to re-arrange, but to remove all things from your life that aren't necessary. Do you really need six cookie sheets, ten casse-role dishes and an infinite number of Tupperware contain-ers? Have your kids outgrown the sipper cups in your cabinets? Do you really still use the twenty-year-old towels your Aunt Martha gave you as a bridal shower gift? (I fi-nally tore mine up to use as cleaning towels and got rid of the bucket of shredded rags I had been using since college. It's amazing how a new cleaning rag can improve my atti-tude when scrubbing the tub!)

How many travel-size bottles of shampoo and lotion do you really need for vacation? Do you really wear all forty sweaters or thirty pairs of shoes? What about those clothes that are a bit (or a lot) too tight? I am a firm be-liever in getting rid of clothes that hurt!

As you move from room to room, think of yourself as a minimalist! If you don't need it, remove it and pass it along to someone who does. Shelters for homeless fami-lies or battered women are in dire need of clothing, household and toiletry items, as well as toys in good con-dition. I suggest calling a few of these organizations and asking them what they need. Their wish list might pro-vide just the motivation to clear away some of the things that are complicating your life.

He who is kind to the poor lends to the LORD,
and he will reward him for what he has done.
(Proverbs 19:17)

Don't Give Up

All hard work brings a profit,
but mere talk leads only to poverty. (14:23)

Avoid the trap of good intentions by getting started right away! I suggest spending one hour each day clearing out your home. If you don't have an hour, commit to fifteen or thirty minutes. Since you are basically sorting your stuff into containers, any amount of time will make a dent.

I suggest scheduling a time when you have a bit of energy and setting a timer. Start in one place and work your way around the room. Stop when the timer goes off, put the lid on your containers and stack them in a corner until tomorrow. (I used to toss a quilt over my containers for a decorative touch—sort of a traveling quilt display.)

Work your way through the house, one room at a time, dejunking all closets, shelves, drawers, cabinets, pantries, chests—anywhere you stash your stuff—as you go. Don't forget the tops of your cabinets, appliances and counters. A good trick is to clear everything (even the coffeemaker) from your counters for a week. (You will not believe how easy it is keep your counters clean!) Then return only the things to the counter that you actually use every day. The rest can be put away in one of your newly cleaned-out cabinets, or, better yet, put in the "Remove" box. Remember, the fewer things you have, the fewer you have to care for.

If you work faithfully for an hour each day, your home will probably be free of clutter in six to eight weeks.

Once you have accomplished this, you can employ some of the organization and storage techniques described in the next chapter. You will be amazed at how much simpler your life is and the amount of extra time you have. So act on your good intentions, and don't give up.

> *But, alas, the daylight is fading,*
> *and the shadows of the evening grow long.*
> (Jeremiah 6:4)

An Exception

I've been talking pretty tough, hmmm? Actually, I am a softie at heart. I believe there is one exception to removing clutter from our homes. Once a child "graduates" from kindergarten, I no longer think we should help de-junk their rooms. What may be clutter or just plain trash to me, can be treasures to my children. If we insist their rooms be free of what we consider clutter, we may be raising a new generation of pack rats.

Now, I am not talking about overlooking health hazards or issuing an open invitation for six-legged pests to take up residence in your child's room. I require my children to remove any dirty dishes from their rooms and empty their trash cans on a regular basis. I also require that there be a path through the room so I don't break my ankle if I have to venture in.

If asked, I will help my children organize their rooms. And, since I've found that my children pay a lot more attention to what I do than what I say, I try to model a fairly clutter-free lifestyle in the rest of the house. It is amazing to see the totally different personalities emerge in the way my children keep their rooms. With one, I want to brag to the grandparents. Another gives me the urge to light a scented candle. Instead, I've learned to bite my tongue and shut the door.

Fathers, do not exasperate your children; instead, bring them up in the training and instruction of the Lord. (Ephesians 6:4)

Practice Restraint

Great job! You did it! Hooray! Hold on! Now that your closets, drawers, cabinets and surfaces are clearer, it may be tempting to fill them up again. Don't. Before you buy anything, I strongly suggest asking yourself three questions:

1. Do I really need it?
2. If so, how and when will I use/wear it?
3. Do I have a place to store it?

Even if you determine you really do have a need for this item and have definite plans to use it, don't bring it home until you have asked and answered that most important question. Everything doesn't always have to be in it's place, but it needs a place. Do not bring anything into your home until you have a definite place to store it.

Have the wisdom to show restraint and, I guarantee, you will be able to find your shoes!

Going Deeper

1. Do you consider yourself or another family member to be a pack rat? What are some of the reasons we find

it hard to let go of our possessions, even if they are complicating our lives?

2. What things are you hanging on to that you really should or could get rid of?

3. Read the account of Esau's relocation in Genesis 36:6-8. What forced Esau to move away from his brother Jacob? In what ways do too many possessions complicate our lives today?

4. Read Ecclesiastes 5:13. What impact does hoarding possessions have upon an individual? What evidence of this truth do you see in our world today?

5. Read Proverbs 21:13 and 19:17. What are the consequences of hoarding possessions when someone less fortunate could make better use of them? Share with each other the needs of your church and other charitable organizations in your community. How could you help?

6. Read Matthew 6:26. What should be our attitude regarding possessions? How can we practically apply this verse to our lives?

7. Read Philippians 4:8. Use this verse to evaluate the possessions in your home (e.g., videotapes, books, clothing, etc.). How can possessions cloud our thinking?

8. Read Ephesians 6:4. What are some ways we can teach our children a proper attitude regarding possessions without exasperating them?

9. Try this exercise. As you enter a room, ask God to give you the wisdom to discern and strength to remove anything that is not glorifying to Him. What was the result?

10. Read Proverbs 14:23. What will you reap through the hard work of loosening your grip on possessions?

CHAPTER THREE

Creating Order – Room by Room

For God is not a God of disorder but of peace. (1 Corinthians 14:33)

Creating Order—Room by Room

A few years ago, if someone had asked me for a word that meant the opposite of disorder, I doubt peace would have come to mind. I definitely had a grasp on the meaning of disorder. I was living in the midst of it. But I had never associated order with peace.

While studying First Corinthians chapter 14 one morning, I used my dictionary to clarify the meaning of verse 33. To my surprise, disorder is actually defined as a breach of peace. Next, I looked up the meaning of peace and found that it is defined as a state of calm and quiet. In those few words, the Bible taught me that bringing order to my home would also bring the peace I craved.

In the last few years, I've found that the efficient organization of my home removes much of the stress that can plague me and my family on a daily basis. As a society, I don't think we realize how much stress we're living under until it's gone. For example, when I worked outside of the home, the daily commute through morning rush hour was an annoyance, but not a big deal. I was used to it.

After a few months of working from home, where my daily commute was from the coffeepot to the computer, the occasional times I needed to venture out during morning or afternoon traffic were extremely stressful. Even though my husband teased me, if a certain activity couldn't be done between 9:30 a.m. and 3:30 p.m., I avoided it like the plague! I think the same principle applies to our home lives.

For many years, I was used to sifting through a huge stack of paper to find a registration form, or digging through the pile of laundry to find the basketball uniform my son needed in fifteen minutes. Chaos was a given. As God helped me create order in my home, room by room, it was as if a huge weight was gradually being lifted from my shoulders. I now know this was the weight of living outside of God's will by not taking the time to learn and heed His ways. Just like I avoid rush hour, I depend on God each day to keep me from slipping back into a life of disorder.

> *Take my yoke upon you and learn from me, for I am gentle and humble in heart, and you will find rest for your souls. For my yoke is easy and my burden is light.* (Matthew 11:29-30)

Freedom!

An organized and orderly home brings freedom to our family, leaving our hearts and minds open to embrace the important things God brings our way. If I'm not spending ten minutes looking for shoes and another ten minutes looking for my car keys, I have an extra twenty minutes in my day to

- share a cup of coffee with my husband . . .
- spark up a conversation with my teenage son . . .
- apply some polish to my daughter's fingernails . . .
- or chat on the phone with a friend.

Taking time for people has eternal value. Frantically searching for your car keys each morning does not.

> *But store up for yourself treasures in heaven.* (Matthew 6:20)

Simplicity

> *God made man simple; man's complex problems are of his own devising.* (Ecclesiastes 7:29, JB)

Simplicity is key to creating order in your home. As you tackle each problem area, ask God to show you the simplest means to the desired end. For example, in the kitchen, store pots near the stove, perhaps on a rack that makes it easy to grab the right size when you need it. Keep fresh towels in each bathroom. Store current magazines near a favorite chair. To those last comments, my daughter would say "Duh!" But for some people, this can be difficult to grasp. I am a prime example.

I used to keep my coffeemaker on the counter, my coffee mugs in a cabinet with the glasses and the coffee and filters in the pantry across the room. My organizing rationale was to store like with like. Make sense? I thought so.

Well, every time my mother-in-law would visit, she would open the cabinet above the coffeemaker looking for the coffee and filters. This just happened to be the cabinet where I kept my mixing bowls. Why keep the mixing bowls in this particular cabinet? I have no idea. It's just where I happened to put them when we moved into the house. (Maybe I didn't have to adjust the shelf for them to fit.)

Later, I noticed that my father-in-law always opened the cabinet above the coffeemaker before he would ask me where we kept the coffee mugs. When we visited my in-laws home, I noticed they kept the coffee, filters and mugs in one cabinet—right above the coffeemaker. This made the process of preparing and serving a pot of coffee much easier. Duh!

I may be a slow learner, but this little coffee drama made me rethink how I stored and organized things in my home. For example, it always annoyed me when the kids would use beach towels for bath towels. Not only were the beach towels in the dirty laundry when it was time to head for the pool, but we didn't want to use them in public anyway. They were extremely faded and worn from so many washings. When I replaced the beach towels, I began to store them away from the bathroom in the hall linen closet. The problem was solved.

Another example is the storage for the shower necessities. I was in the habit of storing extra soap, shampoo and razors on a supply shelf in the hall. Unfortunately, it took me years of emerging from the shower and tiptoeing down the hall dripping wet to grab a bar of soap from the closet before I began to wake up. Today, extra soap, shampoo and razors are stored within reach of each shower—and the hall carpet is dry.

Here's my point, and an important principle in effective home organization. Think about those little annoyances in your home (excluding the kids or the dog). Then ask yourself what you can do to streamline or simplify the area or activity in your home. The answer will invariably lead you to order.

A Place for Everything . . .

The second key to creating order in your home is having a convenient place for everything. Every *thing* may not always be in its place at all times, but you must have a place for it. If you don't have a place for a certain item, get rid of it or something else. As I've said before, it is highly unlikely that your problem is a lack of storage. It is much more likely you simply have too much stuff.

Here's some criteria for assigning a convenient place for your things. The location should be

- near where you will be using it
- easy to access (especially if used a lot)
- must not interfere with other activities.

For example, I store spices near the stove because that's where I generally use them. I try to keep my counter as clear as possible to provide a generous work area and make it easy to clean. I also avoid storing things in the very back of cabinets, since it is difficult to reach and pull things from the back of a cabinet. (You may be able to solve this problem by installing a pull-out rack or bin. You might also try placing a two- to three-inch piece of wood or dense styrofoam in the rear of a cabinet to provide a little platform. This makes it easier to see and retrieve items in the back.)

As you begin to create order, keep your eyes on the goals—simplicity and convenience.

Organizational Tools and Traps

There are many wonderful organizational tools on the market today. You can find them in department stores, home specialty stores, hardware stores, discount stores and catalogs. I've included a helpful listing of the mail-order sources in the resources section at the back of the book.

My favorite organizational tools are pull-out wire baskets, drawer dividers and hooks of all sizes. I use a pull-out wire basket under the kitchen sink to hold our trash sack and am seriously considering asking my husband to install one for recyclables. I have a divider designed especially for the junk drawer, complete with labeled compartments for everything from scotch tape to safety pins. And I don't know what I would do without hooks! We have hooks conveniently placed all over the house for jackets, brooms, bicycles, hairdryers—you name it.

I want to pause here a moment for a reality check. I am not suggesting that you go out and purchase a carload of tools and gadgets to organize your home. You may already have the tools you need. For example, shoe boxes can be used to corral a whole host of things from cosmetics to sales receipts. Cardboard shoe boxes can also be trimmed to fit in drawers. Empty margarine tubs also make great drawer dividers. Old ice cube trays are a great way to organize jewelry. And the zipper bags that often come with blankets are a great place to store off-season sweaters, etc. These are just a few examples. Ask God to stretch your imagination, and you'll be surprised at what you can recycle.

A word of caution. With more and more people trying to restore order to their chaotic lives, organizational tools and techniques have become big business. You can't pass a magazine stand without headlines promising the latest organizational and storage tips. While there are many helpful tools in stores and catalogues, it is easy to go overboard. What is meant to simplify can end up complicating. Remember, the tool should make your life easier, not make you a slave to the system.

Room by Room Strategies

It is time for you to act. . . . (Psalm 119:126)

Now that you have removed many of the things you don't use or need from your home and learned that the keys to creating order are simplicity and convenience, you have the opportunity to employ some organizational strategies to simplify your life. In other words, this is the fun part! I can say this because, in my experience, the rewards of your work in this area are immediate. You now have the opportunity to be a little creative in exploring, experimenting and fine-tuning systems to meet the needs of your family. I encourage you to approach this process both prayerfully and progressively.

Kitchen

Most women spend a lot of time in the kitchen, and I think this time should be as painless as possible. This is probably why I recommend beginning the process of creating order in the kitchen.

So, keeping in mind the principle of storing things where you use them, take a good look around your kitchen. Do you have things organized in a way that makes your kitchen a convenient place to work—and clean up? If not, I strongly encourage you to begin making changes.

Here are my favorite tips for creating order in the kitchen:

- Remove anything from your counter that you don't use every day. The joy of a clear counter is inexpressible!

- Don't overfill cabinets and drawers. Make sure pots, dishes, utensils, etc. are easy to find and re- move when you need them.

- What you don't absolutely need, remove. Also, remove those things that you only use occasion- ally (extra dishes, serving trays, Christmas cookie cutters, ice cream maker, etc.) and store them elsewhere.

- Consider installing a set of shelves near the kitchen (perhaps in the garage) to hold small ap- pliances, large pots, extra supplies, etc.

- Organize your cabinets or pantry by type of food (canned goods, breakfast food, baking supplies, etc.). Label shelves to help family members put away groceries.

- Install pull-out wire bins in lower cabinets. This makes it a snap to find and reach things in the back.

- Store trays and cookie sheets vertically. (If you have space in a cabinet, you might try using a dish drainer to hold them in place.)

- Use dividers in silverware and utensil drawers to separate tools and make them easier to find. The expandable kind make the most efficient use of space.

- You might also put your most frequently used utensils in a pretty crock or clay pot on the countertop.

- Mount a spice rack near the stove, or write the name of the spices on the lids and store them alphabetically in a drawer.
- Adjustable stair-step spice organizers which fit in cabinets also work well.
- Keep your coffee mugs and supplies in a cabinet near the coffeepot; place a towel rack near the sink; hang pot holders by the stove; store placemats and napkins near the table.

    Are you getting the idea?

- Fill a pretty basket with fresh fruit and place it on your counter. Family members will be more likely to grab a healthy snack.
- Store baskets on the top of cabinets or hang them on walls or from a ceiling rack. (A friend of mine hung an antique ladder—horizontally with chains—over her kitchen island with hooks to hang baskets and pots. It not only looks wonderful, but it's also extremely functional.)
- Use sliding bins under your sink to keep trash and recyclables convenient, but out of sight.
- Use the inside of upper cabinets to post important phone numbers, schedules, emergency ingredient substitutions, etc.
- Mount tools such as lid holders or plastic bag storage on the inside of cabinets.

Family Room

This is the room where our family chooses to relax. My goal is to make sure this gathering place is warm and cozy. I want it to be the kind of place that makes you want to put your feet up and let go of the cares of the day and the world.

To cultivate this mood, the sofa and chairs are arranged to encourage conversation. We've installed bookshelves to hold our favorite books and a basket for current magazines. A chess set is always ready to go (although it's been getting pretty dusty these days). In the evening, I'll often light the fireplace or several candles to warm things up. The goal is to create a place of comfort and a much needed spot to unwind.

Here are some tips for keeping your cozy retreat in order:

- I've found baskets of all sizes are great organizers in the family room. For example, a large willow laundry basket can hold quilts and throws and a smaller basket is a great container for TV, VCR and stereo remote controls.

- I keep a basket in the corner as temporary storage for toys. This makes it easy to quickly clean up the room. Make sure your children clean the basket out and put the toys in their permanent storage places at least once a week. Otherwise the basket becomes a clutter magnet.

- Make a habit of tossing old issues of magazines and newspapers as you bring in the new ones, even if you haven't had a chance to read them. This practice will help you form the habit of promptly reading those things you subscribe to or canceling the subscription. (I know, I know. You haven't had a chance to pull out all the good recipes! I suggest chalking this up to another good intention gone bad and let it go. Next time, tear out that great recipe as soon as you see it and slip it in a folder with other recipes you would like to try.)

- Organize books on shelves by subject. This comes with a stern warning. Too many books can become an albatross—or a dust magnet! I strongly suggest giving books away that you are not likely to read again (even if they are hard cover). For example, you might donate Christian books to your church library. This gives others a chance to enjoy the books, and you can always check them out if you would like to read them again.

- Use the same principle to organize VCR tapes, cassettes and CDs by type or subject as you would for books. You can also purchase special cabinets or racks to help store these items neatly. If you, or a member of your family, are the type of people who are more likely to leave CDs, etc., out rather than taking the time to put them back into a storage rack, a basket might be a better choice. Just toss and go!

- An antique trunk or chest can do double duty as a coffee table and extra storage for blankets or other bulky things.

Bathrooms

Personally, I think most people (myself included) store too much stuff in their bathrooms. For example, I used to keep all of our medicine and first-aid supplies in the bathroom closet. My reasoning was likely a holdover from childhood: medicines (and related items) belong in the medicine cabinet. It didn't matter that we were rarely in the bathroom when any of these things were needed, or that our house didn't even have a medicine cabinet in any of the bathrooms. I mindlessly made countless unnecessary trips upstairs for pain reliever, cold medicine, thermometers, Band-Aids, etc., because I insisted that medicine should be stored in a medicine cabinet.

The point of my digression is to prompt you to pause before storing anything in the bathroom. Ask yourself, "Does this really have to be stored here, or would life be simpler if we kept it somewhere else?" Taking the time to think about these questions will likely solve many of your bathroom storage problems.

Here are some of the things that have made our bathrooms much more conducive to the activities they are designed for:

- Since a bathroom is designed for bathing, it's a good idea to keep it clean. To simplify this process, keep surfaces (sink, tub, etc.) clear of clutter. This will make cleaning a breeze.

- Use dividers in drawers to organize cosmetics, hair care products, morning medication or vitamins, etc. You can also use baskets or shoe boxes for this purpose in a closet or under the vanity.

- Mount a blow-dryer on the wall. Wall-mounted blow-dryers are available in most discount stores. You can also put up a hook to hang your dryer or curling iron to keep it handy.

- Install pull-out bins or plastic tubs under the sink to organize and store cleaning supplies, bath toys

15

or extra supplies of necessities like toilet paper, shampoo, conditioner, soap, etc.

- Roll towels and place in a large, sturdy basket by the shower or tub. This keeps them handy and saves space in the linen closet. If the basket is large enough, you might slip in an extra bottle of shampoo or bar of soap so these necessities are within easy reach when needed.

- Use a shower or tub organizer for shampoo, conditioner, shower gel, etc. Many different types are available at discount or specialty home stores. A mom I know puts a dish drainer on the floor of the tub/shower combination to corral these items. All ages can reach what they need, it's easy for kids to keep it neat and doesn't fill up with water like some tub caddies.

- Hang a squeegee in the shower and encourage the last person out to wipe down the walls and doors. A towel can also be used, or try one of the clean-shower spray-on products. It's amazing how much work this extra thirty seconds will save when it comes to scrubbing hard-water marks off shower doors and tile. (As annoying as it is for procrastinators like myself, "an ounce of prevention is worth a pound of cure.")

Bedrooms

My husband and I prefer our bedroom to be free of clutter. We rest better when it's that way. Our children are just the opposite. They love to have everything from art supplies to sports equipment right at their fingertips. Maybe they think they will wake up in the middle of the night with an uncontrollable urge to build a tower from Legos.

After several years of unsuccessful attempts at explaining the storage advantages of a closet as opposed to the perimeter of the room or every available surface, my husband and I have decided to allow the children to decorate their rooms in their own style. We know that someday, when turning their bedrooms into spare rooms, we will long for the baseball card collection or row of Beanie Babies lined up along the wall.

Here are a few tips for those who enjoy the serenity of a clutter-free bedroom:

- Beds with comforters are much easier to make than those with bedspreads. Just pull up the comforter, and toss on some decorative throw pillows.

- Put a dust ruffle on your bed, and you no longer have to look at the dust bunnies under the bed. This is also a good place to store out-of-season clothing, extra blankets, etc. You can find containers designed specifically for this purpose at most discount, hardware or home specialty stores.

- A nightstand with drawers is a great place to stow bedtime reading material, medicine, even an extra pair of socks for chilly nights. You can make a quick nightstand by covering an inexpensive round table with a pretty cloth. You'll have a bedside table as well as storage space underneath for nighttime essentials.

- Consider slipping a comfortable chair, small table and lamp in the corner of your bedroom for a cozy retreat. This may become your favorite quiet time spot.

- Put a vase of fresh flowers (from your garden, grocery store or husband) and some scented candles in your bedroom. You will feel relaxed, pampered—and romantic!

As I've said, children's rooms can be a challenge. My first suggestion is to relax your standards a bit, remembering that children are children. They do not think like we do, and they don't seem to mind having crayons and game pieces mixed in with the Legos. With this in mind, I've found that plastic bins of all sizes work well to sort and corral toys, hobbies, collections, art supplies, etc.

You can help your kids learn to keep their things organized by attaching labels or pictures to the bins to help them clean up after playtime. For example, attach a picture of a toy car on a tub that holds the cars and race track. Cut out Barbie's picture from the package and tape it to a tub for dolls and their clothes. Work with them to put away a toy or activity before pulling out a new one.

. . . *pleasant words promote instruction.* (Proverbs 16:21)

Closets

The problem with storing our wardrobes generally hinge on one factor—too many clothes. I remember hearing a Christian speaker saying that her closet should have "those little size rings 8, 10, 12, 14, none of your business. . . ." Mine was no exception. It was extremely painful to part with my used-to-be-favorite pair of jeans or the dress I wore on a special date with my husband. I kept thinking these clothes would come back into style, or that one day I would lose weight and be able to zip my jeans. Although neither of these things happened, I did feel a surprising amount of satisfaction after finally biting the bullet and ruthlessly cleaning out my closet.

So, before you begin to organize your closet, I strongly suggest removing any clothing you haven't worn in the last twelve months. If you aren't ready to part with these clothes, put them in storage. If you haven't worn them in another year, you should now be convinced it's time to get rid of them. Frankly, I still ease myself into parting with clothing by putting anything I haven't worn in a year into a large plastic tub with a lid. I write the date on the tub and keep it on the top shelf of the closet. If I want to wear something, I can easily retrieve it. I don't re-member ever opening up the tub to pull something out, but I have found that it is much easier to get rid of cloth-ing I haven't worn in two years instead of one!

Here are some strategies for organizing your wardrobe once you have gotten rid of the things you don't need:

- Store as much clothing as possible on hangers without stuffing your closet. This makes it easier to find what you need and cuts down on wrinkles.

- I put clothing on hangers immediately from the dryer and try to touch up anything that needs ironing right way. A pull-down ironing center mounted on the wall or door of a walk-in closet is extremely handy.

- Replace wire hangers with plastic tube hangers. Plastic hangers are less likely to damage your cloth-ing and do not get tangled in the closet. You might also assign a different color hanger to each family member. This system makes putting clothing away a breeze.

- Consider renovating your closet to provide double racks for short items, space for long items and a vertical stack of shelves. Then, organize clothing according to type. For example, put all skirts in one area, all jackets together, etc. I like to organize shirts by sleeve length, from tank tops to long sleeves.

- Hang trousers from the hem using a skirt hanger rather than folding over a hanger. This keeps wrinkles out, uses less space and pants won't slip off the hanger.

- If you have additional space, move off-season clothing to the side or back of your closet rather than removing it. (Don't do this at the expense of crowding your closet. It's better to take the time to store off-season clothing elsewhere than to struggle with a too-full closet all year long.)

- Our bedroom has a fairly long walk-in closet with racks on either side. We built a wall separating the last third of the closet from the rest, installed a door and lined the walls in the enclosed area with cedar. This makes it easy to move and safely store our off-season wardrobe.

- Use shelves to store folded sweaters, purses, etc. Shelf dividers will help keep these items neatly stacked.

- Install hooks for robes, bags, etc.

- If possible, store luggage on the top shelf of the closet.

69

- Avoid storing shoes on the floor. They are difficult to find and can get lost under hanging clothing. Shoes can be easily organized with an over-the-door shoe rack or hanging bag.
- Organizers are available specifically for ties, scarves, belts, jewelry, etc. There are models for hanging in a closet or placing in drawers.
- Use dividers in drawers to sort underwear, socks, hose, lingerie, etc. Shoe boxes with the sides trimmed, empty diaper wipe containers or plastic bins all work well for this purpose.

Coat Closet

It's embarrassing to admit this, but the biggest challenge with our coat closet was finding room for the coats. This small closet had become a catchall for everything from the vacuum cleaner to my husband's hunting gear. Once we sorted it out and removed extraneous items, we not only had room for our coats, but we even had room for the coats of our guests!

Here are a few tips that have worked well for our family:

- We use the coat closet for our off-season coats or those we don't wear every day. Our everyday coats are hung on hooks near the door. My reasoning is that a hook by the door is more likely to be used by my family than a hanger in the hall closet. This keeps coats from piling up on the floor or backs of chairs. With our "everyday" jackets and coats hung on hooks by the door, the coat closet holds our "dress" coats, off-season jackets, snow pants, boots, scarves, hats and gloves.

- Try using a hanging shoe bag—the kind with the little shelves—to hold mittens, gloves, hats and scarves. (This is my favorite organizational tip because it works so well.)

- Large plastic tubs work well for snowboots and snow pants. These can be stored out of the way on the top shelf or the back of the closet and pulled out when needed.

- If you have small children, mount low hooks so they can hang up their own jackets and backpacks.

- Try to find a new place for the vacuum cleaner. (Unfortunately, mine is still in our coat closet. I am hoping to be inspired with a great place to store the vacuum cleaner before, in frustration, I toss a quilt over it and convince myself it's a clever quilt rack.)

Linen Closet

A linen closet is wonderful. In our home it is used for much more than linens. Here are some of my favorite organizing strategies for linen closets:

- Label the shelves of your linen closet to make things easier to find and to put away. For example, labels may read "queen-sized sheet sets" or "table-cloths." Not only is it easier for you and other family members to find what you need without rooting through the entire closet, but the labels also make it much more likely these items will be put away in the right place. Fold sheet sets, and slip them into the matching pillowcase.

- Put tablecloths and matching napkins together before storing. You might slip them in a large self-sealing bag. Label with size and number of napkins.

- Use your linen closet for extra toiletry supplies such as lotion, deodorant, cotton balls, etc.

Storage Areas—Garage, Basement, Attic

These storage areas may be your biggest challenge. They certainly were mine. Instead of making a decision about whether we really needed to keep something, I would shove it in the storage room. Pretty soon this became so overcrowded that I wondered why I was storing something that I would never be able to find again. That's when things started to overflow to the garage.

With this in mind, I strongly suggest you do a little soul searching before you put anything in storage. Ask yourself, "Do I really need to keep this? If so, will I be able to find it in storage when I need it?" Both answers must be a definite "yes" before even opening the door to your storage room.

It's also important to determine if the item is something for long-term or short-term storage. Long-term storage items might include your wedding dress or the box of baby clothes you can't bear to part with. Short-term storage may include items like camping gear, sports equipment, bicycles, etc. Designating storage items as long-term or short-term will help you decide how and where to store them.

Here are some suggestions to bring order to your storage areas:

- Use large plastic tubs to store things that are moved around a lot, such as camping gear, Christmas decorations, etc. I love these tubs because they are sturdy, stackable, relatively inexpensive and keep the contents clean and dry. You can also use cardboard boxes for storage. If you do, make sure they are very sturdy and approximately the same size so they stack easily. Stacking boxes of all different sizes can really be a waste of space.

- Use smaller tubs or sturdy boxes for heavy items like dishes or books. But first, ask yourself if you really need to keep the books you aren't reading or the dishes you aren't using.

    (I know, it's your mother's china and you can't get rid of it. If these dishes hold special memories, why don't you use them? Or better yet, hand them down to your daughter?)

    (I know, your husband is keeping those boxes of college books in case he needs to look up a law of physics or math equation someday. Why not encourage him to explore the wealth of current information available on the Internet? The Library of Congress is at our fingertips.)

- List the contents on the outside of all storage containers.

- Label shelves to assist in finding items and putting them away.

- Store extra blankets in clear zippered bags or trash bags. Slipping in a dryer sheet will keep them smelling fresh.

- Cover bulky items (high chairs, Christmas trees, etc.) with a large clear plastic trash bag to keep off dust.

- Sort and label outgrown children's clothing (that you plan to use again) with size, gender and season. Only keep the best and store these containers in one area.

- Clean, restock and repair items such as camping gear, Christmas decorations, picnic basket, first-aid kit, etc., before returning to storage. It can spoil a great mood to scrape last year's wax off the Christmas candleholders or pull out a pot and find mold growing on unwashed camping gear.

- Keep as much off the garage floor as possible. Hang bicycles, gardening tools, wagons, wheelbarrows, etc.

- Consider investing in an organizer specifically designed to hold sporting equipment. We have an organizer that hangs on the garage wall with spots for balls (soccer, football, baseball, softball and basketball), bats, hockey sticks, bike helmets, tennis rackets—even a couple of lawn chairs.

- A plastic trash can is a great container for balls. Large plastic tubs also work well to corral all sorts of sports equipment—especially roller blades.

Now, if you want your storage areas to be really organized and are fairly good with a computer word processing program, you might inventory the items in storage in a database. Then use the print/merge function of the program to create a list of contents to help you quickly find something in storage when you need it.

Honestly, I haven't done a computer inventory of the items in our storage areas, but I really like the idea and hope to get around to it someday. If I do, here's how I plan to do it:

1. Set up a database with three columns. Label one column with the "Container #," the second with "Contents" and the last column with "Storage Area."

2. For each container assign a number, label it and record the number in the first column of your database. List the contents in the second column. For example:

CONTAINER #	CONTENTS	STORAGE AREA
1	John's HS Yearbooks & Memories	Basement
2	Camp stove Cooking kit	Garage
3	Christmas tree lights Outdoor lights Advent wreath	Attic

3. Notice that some containers can be identified with a general title, but with others it's better to be more specific. For example, you may need the Advent wreath from Container #3 but aren't ready to put up decorations quite yet. Generally, the more specific you are when listing the contents of the containers, the better.

4. Once you have completed your inventory of all the containers you have in storage, use the print/merge

function to produce labels listing the number and contents for each one. Secure these to your containers.

5. Next, print out several copies of the complete database. Place a copy in your household file, and post one in each of your storage areas (basement, garage, attic, etc.). Now, when you need to find something, you can consult your inventory list and know just how to find the item. (You may also want to place a copy of your inventory in a safe deposit box. It could come in handy if you need to file an insurance claim for lost or damage goods.)

This system, I confess, is just a good intention right now in our home. However, when John asks me where the Christmas lights are, I would love to replace "Your guess is as good as mine" with something like "Just a moment, sweetheart. Let me consult the storage inventory. Yes, here they are. You can find them in the container labeled #3 on the third shelf of the storage room"—and then watch him keel over!

Order = Peace = Joy

I began this chapter with First Corinthians 14:33, "For God is not a God of disorder but of peace." My prayer is that you will go to God, the God of peace, and ask Him to show you how to create the order He desires for your home. Remember, don't strive for perfection; strive for simplicity. The resulting peace will bring true joy as you are linked with God in your ministry to your family and others.

> . . . *the joy of the LORD is your strength.* (Nehemiah 8:10)

Going Deeper

1. What emotions do a disorderly home evoke in you? What is it like living in a disorderly home?
2. What are the benefits of order in a home? Share a personal example of how order in a certain area has made a positive impact in your life.
3. Read First Corinthians 14:33. What are some other instances in Scripture that prove the truth of this verse that God values order? Why do you think this is so?
4. Use a dictionary to define disorder and peace. Why does God contrast these two words in First Corinthians 14:33? How does this apply to your home?
5. Read First Corinthians 4:2. With what have you been entrusted? How can disorder in our lives prevent us from being good stewards of God's gifts?
6. Read Proverbs 15:22. Spend some time sharing your challenges as well as successful strategies for bringing order to the following areas of your home: kitchen, family room, bathroom, bedrooms, closets, storage areas, children's areas.
7. Identify one area of your home that would benefit from more order. Commit to seeking God's help to bring order to this area. What were the results?

CHAPTER FOUR

The
Paper
Chase

I have found the Book of the Law in the temple of the LORD. (2 Kings 22:8)

The Paper Chase

One of my biggest challenges is dealing with the mountain of paper that comes into our home on a daily basis—mail, school papers, magazines, catalogs (which seem to increase each day like the mint that is taking over my garden), bills, photographs, children's artwork—you name it. My problem is sorting the important from the not-so-important and making sure I can find the really important stuff when we need it.

I really used to beat myself up about how I managed paper flow in our home. I'd start sorting through a pile and say to myself, "It can't be that hard to keep track of the school lunch menu, spelling words, insurance statements, coupons, photos . . . " until I had worn myself out just thinking about what to do with the pile. It was much easier to put it all in a basket on top of the refrigerator or in a cabinet or in the laundry room or. . . . This was the crux of my problem—trying to guess in which pile I would find what I needed.

> *All Scripture is God-breathed and is useful for teaching, rebuking, correcting and training in righteousness.*
> (2 Timothy 3:16)

The Bible is so precious to me, and one of the reasons is because it is so practical! Who would think I would find encouragement (and conviction) regarding my per-

Making Your Home a Haven

sonal paper chase while reading about the history of Israel in Second Kings 22 and 23? I didn't even think they
had paper back then! I found in my study of these chapters that even the temple priests had trouble keeping
track of the really important paper that came their way.
Let me give you a synopsis of these chapters.

One of the first major decisions eighteen-year-old
Josiah made as King of Judah was to order repairs to the
temple. When the priests started cleaning up and sorting
through their piles, they were surprised to discover the
Book of the Law (the only copy) buried under a pile of
debris. (Sound familiar?) The Book of the Law had been
missing for many, many years, so many years that people
had completely forgotten what it said.

Now, remember, this wasn't just any book. This was
God's revelation to Moses—The Law—found in the
first five chapters of the Bible. God gave very specific instructions in these Books about all aspects of life for His
chosen people from how to worship to how to treat your
mother and father. This was important stuff!

I can just imagine the panic of the priest who had originally misplaced the Book of the Law. "I left it right here
on the counter yesterday! Where could it be? I thought it
was right here in this pile! Maybe I put it in the closet."
After a while, the priest probably convinced himself he
didn't really need the Book of the Law. He could remember what it said (or at least the gist of it).

Now, centuries later under the reign of Josiah, both
the priests and the people had completely forgotten
God's Law and were living "as they saw fit." They had
even put some statues of other gods in the temple and
had begun to practice astrology. When the assistant

priest, Hilkiah, discovers the Book, he brings it to the head priest.

"I have found the Book of the Law in the temple of the LORD" (22:8) he says. The head priest reports this discovery to King Josiah.

"Hilkiah the priest has given me a book" (22:10) (almost as if he wasn't sure what it was). Then he starts to read from it—and was Josiah in for a surprise!

> *When the king heard the words of the Book of the Law, he tore his robes. He gave these orders to Hilkiah the priest . . . "Great is the LORD's anger that burns against us because our fathers have not obeyed the words of this book; they have not acted in accordance with all that is written there concerning us." (22:11-13)*

The story concludes with Josiah gathering all the people together as he reads the Book to them.

> *The king stood by the pillar and renewed the covenant in the presence of the LORD—to follow the LORD and keep his commands, regulations and decrees with all his heart and all his soul, thus confirming the words of the covenant written in this book. Then all the people pledged themselves to the covenant. (23:3)*

So, what piece of paper have you misplaced lately that was really important?

A Wake-up Call

Dealing with paper is a huge challenge for most families, ours included. At one time, I used to stack all my paper in pretty Longenberger baskets thinking it wasn't really a mess if it was in a $50 basket. As the baskets filled, I bought more and moved them to the top of the refrigerator, to a closet and to the basement shelves. It took losing my husband's year-end bonus check before I woke up (as I'm sure the temple priests did) and realized I needed to find a better way to organize the paper that was streaming into our home.

On the following pages, I share my method for dealing with paper. I hope you will find it useful. Although I am confident you will benefit from many of the principles, my method may not suit the needs of your family. The key is to pray about your struggle and trust God to help you find the system that works best for you. Place your baskets of paper at His feet and ask Him to help you sort out the mess—then avoid filling them up again.

Do It Now

There are some things where the consequences of a little procrastination are not dire. Dealing with paper is not one of them! We cannot let paper pile up even a little bit. Personally, I am convinced that paper has a life of its own and secretly multiplies overnight. (In fact, I am just about ready to subscribe to the notion that today's paper has a mutant gene causing unexplained, but rapid, cloning.) Make it a habit to deal with this menace as soon as it comes into your home.

The way to bring order to paper quickly and efficiently is to have a place for every kind, a convenient place, and put it in this place as soon as it comes into the house. You can use cubbyholes in a desk, file folders in a box or cabinet, envelopes—whatever works best for you. The key comes from Nike: "Just do it!"

I've found that a file box (or crate) with hanging folders of different colors works best. Label your file folders with the following categories:

- Do
- Pay
- File
- Read
- School
- Husband
- Coupons
- Memories (one folder for each family member)

As soon as you take the mail from your box, open your child's backpack or peruse that packet of newly developed photos, start sorting. In fact, I am now in the habit of doing a quick sort before I walk in the door and find that at least half of the paper doesn't even make it into the house. Here's how:

- In your "Do" folder, place all pieces of paper that serve as reminders of things you need to do. For example, this is the place I put wedding invitations or graduation announcements to remind me to send a gift. (It's important to first note the date on your calendar if you will be attending the ceremony.) I might also place a letter that I would like to reply to in this folder or slip a note to myself such as a reminder to send a thank-you card or return an item.

- The "Pay" folder is pretty obvious. This is the place for bills that need to be paid. I have a friend who makes her check out right away and writes the date due where the stamp will be placed. I haven't reached that point of organization yet. Our bills go into the folder until our "paper purge," which is a scheduled time twice a month when we pay bills as well as tackle the "Do" and "File" folders.

- The "File" folder is the place for the things that you need to keep, but require no action. These include tax records, warranty booklets, vacation information, financial statements, insurance policies, utility stubs, etc. When this type of paper comes into the house, I do not file it in our permanent household file right away, although that could be done. I have found it easier to do filing all at once at the conclusion of the "paper purge."

A word about a regular "paper purge." This system is a form of "planned procrastination." Some efficiency experts say that you should handle a piece of paper just one time. To this I respond, "Yeah, right!" I realize that I don't have the time or the inclination to deal fully with all the paper that comes into our home immediately. But, until my "paper purge," I know basically where to look for it.

A word of caution. This system will fall apart very quickly if you don't schedule a "paper purge." Your temporary files will quickly turn into just another set of piles if you don't put this time on your calendar and stick to the commitment. If necessary, bribe yourself (and/or your husband) with a treat during this time to make sure you show up at the "office."

- The "Read" folder is the place for the things that come into the house that you may want to read, but don't have time at the moment. This may include the newsletters from various organizations such as your church or school. Or it might be a booklet outlining benefit changes from your or your husband's employer. I sometimes tear out an article from a newspaper or magazine and slip it in this folder to read later.

  I frequently use my scheduled "paper purge" to go through this folder and stash this reading material in various places where I am likely to have the time to read it. For example, I always keep a few things in the car to read while I wait for Liz at soccer practice or in the parking lot while I wait to pick up Freddy after school. I may throw an item or two in my purse to read while waiting in lines or at the doctor's office. Try to be alert to times when you are waiting. It is a good time to tackle your "Read" file.

  When my kids were small, I would put things from this folder in the bathroom to read while they bathed. I am now at the point in my life where my kids can take their own showers, and I can take guilt-free time for a leisurely bath to catch up on my "Read" file.

- The "School" folder is for school information or papers you may need to keep handy for a short period of time. It may contain this week's spelling words or the

list of things to bring for a school party. I suggest sign-
ing permission slips or filling out other communication with the school right away and slipping it in your
child's backpack. I have been caught too many times,
in the past, having to run the money or permission
slip up to school at the last minute for a field trip. I
have learned my lesson. Do it now!

Anna informed me recently that her second-grade
teacher will make her put her name in "The Book" if
she doesn't return her Friday folder each week. I
don't know about you, but I certainly don't want to
face the wrath of a second grader on Friday afternoon
with her name in "The Book."

- The "Husband" folder. Ah! This is always a challenge for me. I used to leave my husband's personal
mail on the kitchen counter so he could go
through it after work. Often after looking over his
mail, he would leave it on the counter or place it in
one of those now empty $50 baskets—and there it
rested permanently. Now, after he has looked at it,
I put it in his folder. He knows where to look if he
needs it—and I have my baskets back.

Just the other day, John asked where his eyeglass
prescription form was. It was much more pleasant
to say, "I bet it's in your folder," than "How am I
supposed to know?" This kind of response helps
me worry a little less concerning that verse in Proverbs about it being "[b]etter to live in a desert than
with a quarrelsome and ill-tempered wife" (Proverbs 21:19).

- The "Coupon" file. Frankly, I am not a big coupon saver. I used to be, but the coupons always seemed to expire before I remembered to use them. Now, I save a few coupons, generally for dry cleaning, pizza, videos and the Christian bookstore. If I am going to use these right away, I slip them in my purse. If not, they go in this folder.

  If you use coupons regularly, you might take a look at some of the special coupon organizers on the market. There are even some that look like a wallet that you can bring to the store. I have a friend who uses a small file box to sort her coupons. She organizes the different categories (cereal, diapers, cleaning products, etc.) in order of expiration date with the ready-to-expire in front. She brings the entire box to the store and sets it up in the child seat of the cart so her coupons are at her fingertips. That's organization!

  If you like to clip coupons, I suggest finding a gadget or system that is simple and convenient. Definitely don't toss them unsorted into an old shoe box like I used to do.

- The "Memory" file. The first time I spoke to a group of women about home organization and management, I was asked a question about what I did with the photos and "memories" that came into the house. I looked at the woman who had asked the question rather blankly and said, "You know, our photos and memories are stuffed in a big box in my basement. That's not much of a system, is it?"

By then, I had learned to be alert for the promptings of the Holy Spirit and felt this was an area of my home God might want to help me improve. But, when I looked at the enormity of the task, I was immobilized. Thankfully, I had learned that the best thing to do when I feel frightened and overwhelmed is to pray. In answer to my prayers, God inspired me with a great idea that has turned into a marvelous system and tradition for our family. It is amazing what God can do with a little raw material and a willing spirit.

In addition to inspiration, He provided a block of time to tackle the giant box (and as I later discovered, numerous grocery bags) filled with everything from baby booties to school pictures. My children had been invited to spend a week at the farm with their grandparents, so I had an entire week without the responsibility for their care. After a day or so, I began to miss them, and that's when the inspiration came to begin sifting through "the box." This project took me all week. I even worked until 2 a.m. one evening. (After all, Freddy was ten years old by now, and I hadn't even finished his baby book!)

By the time the children returned, I had not only finished the baby books, but I had also assembled a scrapbook full of photos and memories for each child. These scrapbooks were placed in large plastic tubs (labeled with each child's name) along with other memories like their baby books, a few special items of clothing or toys and some artwork. I even tied up the cards and letters each child had received over the years from friends and relatives with a ribbon and placed them in the memory tub. I also put together school scrapbooks that I had purchased years earlier for each child, but were just collecting dust. These books were the perfect place for the yearly school pictures, report cards and a few special papers and artwork completed during the year.

Today, scrapbooking is extremely popular. There are a variety of scrapbook supplies available from specialty, craft or discount stores or through individual home sales representatives. Unfortunately, I am not very artistic or "crafty" and didn't worry too much about how creative my books were when I first put them together. I was more interested in just getting them done! Regardless, my children were delighted by their scrapbooks and memory tubs when they returned from the farm. They still frequently page through them.

Now, throughout the year, I save ticket stubs, vacation information, school pictures, letters, a few pieces of artwork or papers and photos. In my file box, each family member has a file folder labeled with their name. I also have one labeled "Others." I use the folders to hold these memories and photos (I always get doubles) during the year. On New Year's Day, we have a tradition of updating our scrapbooks and memory tubs. Everyone just grabs his folder from the file box and updates his own book. It provides a wonderful opportunity to look back over the year and thank God for the special times and memories He has given us individually, and as a family.

My children love their memory tubs. I love them too. Memories and tradition are extremely important to children. Experts say cultivating traditions is one of the ways to build a strong family. I want to encourage you to ask God to help you preserve these special times and events by bringing order to that big box in your basement.

Simplicity Is the Key

As you seek God's direction in developing a system to help you manage the paper that comes into your home, remember to keep His wise words in mind:

God made man simple; man's complex problems are of his own devising. (Ecclesiastes 7:29, JB)

In our zeal to bring order to the piles of paper in our homes, we run the risk of setting up a system that complicates our lives rather than making it easier. I am a prime example. A few years ago, we purchased money management software intended to simplify our record keeping, bill paying, etc. The system was so overwhelming to me that I put off balancing our checkbook for an entire year! In all fairness, this same software has helped many people I know, but for me it was an albatross. I have recently discovered, however, that automatic payment of regular bills (mortgage, utilities, etc.) and using Internet banking has really streamlined my work in this area. Just remember, it is not the system that works, it's God working to bring order to your life. Seek Him, and allow Him to help you put an end to your own "paper chase."

*Praise the LORD . . . who redeems your life from the pit
and crowns you with love and compassion.*
(Psalm 103:2, 4)

Going Deeper

1. Why do you think we have so much trouble keeping track of the paper that comes into our homes? What are your biggest challenges when it comes to chasing paper?
2. What piece of paper have you misplaced that was really important?
3. Read Second Kings 22 and 23. What had been lost? What was the result of this loss? How can losing track of paper disrupt your family life?
4. What are the principles for dealing with paper in an orderly way?
5. What system do you use to organize the paper coming into your home? What works well? Where might you make improvements? Share your questions and ideas with the group.
6. Why is it important to preserve photos and memorabilia? What are the challenges to this endeavor? Share some strategies for preserving memories that have worked well for you.
7. Read Psalm 44:1-3. How may we preserve a record of how God has worked in our family's lives today?

8. Identify and address a paper challenge in your life. Share the results.

CHAPTER FIVE

Managing
Your
Time

Give careful thought to your ways. You have planted much, but have harvested little. (Haggai 1:5-6)

Managing Your Time

There are days when Haggai 1:5-6 describes me to a "T." At the end of one of these days, I wonder where my time has gone. I can't seem to accomplish anything. I try so hard, but my time just slips away. Fortunately, these days have been popping up less and less as I give up my planner and let the ultimate time management expert teach me His ways. After all, He is the One who managed to create the entire universe in six days. I guess He has a few things to teach us about using our time wisely.

Just as I need to identify my sin to be able to turn from it, God impressed upon me that the first step to becoming a good steward of my time involved trying to figure out where I was spending it. After much internal debate and weeks of procrastination, I decided the best way to do this was to spend a week tracking every hour of my day and recording how I spent my time. This was extremely painful, but so eye-opening.

Through this exercise, I found I spent much more time thinking about and talking about doing laundry than actually doing it. I also found myself at the grocery store six to eight times a week. While I had frequently described myself as a "morning person," I found that I rarely got up before 7:30 a.m. I also realized I spent more time getting ready to work at my public relations business (cleaning off my desk, making coffee, talking on the phone) than actually working.

This was not a pretty picture. But at least now I knew where my time was going, and I was ready to make some changes. Through persistent prayer that "not my will, but Thine be done," God created in me a commitment to truly "give careful thought to my ways" and strive to be a good steward of my time.

Setting Goals

Just as it's difficult to run a race with no idea of the location of the finish line, you can't run through your day with no idea where you need to end up. Prayerful goal setting is crucial.

I don't have time to set goals! I hardly have time to sort the socks! you are probably thinking. I understand. You must know by now that I've been in the same place. In fact, I still struggle every day to use my time wisely. I've learned that, as exasperating as it may be, goal setting is crucial.

Ask any successful business person about the importance of setting goals. (Now, you are probably thinking, *I don't have time to talk to some successful business person—the soup is burning!*) But many of the same principles apply for work at home as they do in the office. It is crucial to identify where you want to go and make a plan to get there. If you don't, you will end up just as the verse in Haggai describes, "[planting] much and [harvesting] little."

The first step in goal setting is to come together as a family and prayerfully discuss and develop a mission statement. Why does your family exist? What is your purpose both individually and as a family unit? You might draw your mission statement from the Great Commission Jesus gave to His disciples before ascending into heaven.

> *Therefore go and make disciples of all nations, baptizing them in the name of the Father and of the Son and of the Holy Spirit, and teaching them to obey everything I have commanded you.* (Matthew 28:19-20)

A mission statement drawn from these verses might read something like: "The mission of the _____ family, individually and corporately, is to be willing, equipped and available to make disciples for Jesus Christ."

Next, develop a list of goals and strategies which flow from this mission statement. For example, a family goal might be: "Grow in our relationship with God." Strategies under this goal might include, "Attend worship together each week." "Participate in family devotions." "Pray together as a family each day."

Another family goal might be: "Care for our bodies so we may have 'strong arms' for God's work." Strategies under this goal may include, "Prepare and eat healthy meals." "Participate in a family exercise activity once a week." Get the idea?

Once you have committed your mission statement, goals and strategies to paper, use this document to evaluate your schedule. Now comes the truly difficult part. Eliminate those activities that do not help you achieve the goals you have set individually and as a family.

> *Therefore be careful how you walk, not as unwise men, but as wise, making the most of your time.* (Ephesians 5:15-16, NASB)

I really feel that one of Satan's most effective tools for keeping us from God and breaking down families is our own busyness. When we reach burnout from all our frantic running to and fro (and we will), Satan has us right where he wants us—tired, frustrated, depleted. We do not have the strength or the vision to resist temptation, regardless of the consequences.

I encourage you to take a good, long, prayerful look at your schedule. Do your children have to be involved in so many activities? Do you have to be involved in so many organizations or agree to help on so many committees? What can you eliminate that is putting stress on your family? Answer these questions honestly and prayerfully, and then start pruning.

The Early Bird Catches the Worm (and other truths that are a lot harder to swallow than a worm)

God has a lot to say about getting up early. Frankly, I was shocked! I used to think He uniquely created us as "morning people" or "night owls." I've changed my mind after reading what He has to say about getting up early. Just listen to this:

How long will you lie there, you sluggard?
When will you get up from your sleep? (Proverbs 6:9)

As a door turns on its hinges,
so a sluggard turns on his bed. (26:14)

A little sleep, a little slumber,
a little folding of the hands to rest—

> *and poverty will come on you like a bandit*
> *and scarcity like an armed man.* (6:10-11)

> *A wife of noble character, who can find?*
> *She is worth far more than rubies. . . .*
> *She gets up while it is still dark;*
> *she provides food for her family.* (31:10, 15)

Did you know that God uses the word "sluggard" fourteen times in the book of Proverbs alone? That's only one book of the Bible! God has a lot to say about sleeping late, and it is not good. Proverbs alone was enough evidence for me to ask God to help me truly become a morning person.

I have made it a habit to pray before I go to sleep that God will help me get up on time, at the time I have set aside to spend in quiet time with Him. I set my bedside clock ahead ten minutes to give me that extra leeway when I am tempted to turn in my bed "as the door on its hinges. . . ." Although I occasionally give in to the powerful pull of my "hinges" and roll over, my conscience always "creaks" when I finally get up. So, I encourage fellow "sluggards" to make it a point to catch the beauty of the sunrise and see what a difference it will make in your day!

Divine Intervention

One of the best habits God has helped me develop is the practice of giving Him my day and asking Him to set my "to-do" list. I do this during my morning quiet time.

I ask Him to make His purposes my purposes. I pray for the wisdom and discernment to do what He has for me to do that day. I ask for strong arms to do the work He has planned. And I end by asking Him to help me make the best use of my time and to stretch the hours.

You know what? God always answers this prayer in ways I would have never imagined. It is such fun to see how He so creatively does it. And you know what else? Things tend to work out just right.

> *If their purpose or activity is of human origin, it will fail.* (Acts 5:38)

Quit Procrastinating

> *The wise woman builds her house, but with her own hands the foolish one tears hers down.* (Proverbs 14:1)

No habit will tear your home down more quickly than that of procrastination. The King James Version of the Bible uses the words "plucketh it down" in this verse. I think this is a wonderful word picture—just like plucking feathers—one by one. I've found the habit of procrastination destroys the peace of a home little by little, piece by piece. I have learned this lesson more times than I can remember, sometimes with very dire consequences.

I once returned an electronic item to the store. Even though I had the sales receipt, I could not get a refund because I had put off returning it for several months. And I wish I had a nickel for every time I went to check out books at the library or a movie at the video store and the clerk announced I owed a late fee. I cringe when I think of late fees we have incurred when I failed to mail a check on time, or the many birthdays I missed because I put off sending a card or gift. The casualty list resulting from my habit of procrastination goes on and on.

To help you break this habit, I'll share the strategy that helped me the most to overcome it. First, sit down and make a list of all the things you've been putting off. Then make a commitment to God that you will not go to bed until you can cross one thing off of the list each day or at least complete part of it. Ask for His strength to keep this promise. (Remember John 15:5.) Trust me, you will soon tire of writing an overdue thank-you note to Aunt Martha or hemming your son's pants at midnight. Before you even realize it, your habit of procrastination will be a distant memory.

Now, after you've done those things, instead of resting on your laurels, replace the bad habit of procrastination with new, good habits. For example, get in the habit of doing the most difficult tasks first. (I hate this, but it does work!) Develop a mentality of getting things done now rather than later. I ask the Holy Spirit to bring to mind the Nike slogan whenever I am tempted to procrastinate— "Just Do It!"

Time Savers

[Make] the most of every opportunity. (Colossians 4:5, NASB)

I think saving time is found in the little things, making the most of every opportunity. Much of this comes from developing good habits and letting go of the bad.

When I was learning to change from a "sluggard" to a "morning person," I used to stumble down to the kitchen (while it was still dark . . . thanks to the Proverbs 31 woman) and stare at my coffee while it brewed. It didn't take long for the Holy Spirit to break through the fog and prod me into using those few minutes in a more productive way. Now, I turn on the coffee and resist the urge to watch it brew. Instead, my morning habit is to toss in a load of laundry, empty the dishwasher and take dinner out of the freezer. It's amazing how much I can get done in those six or seven minutes.

In the evening, I make it my habit to pick up the house, look at the calendar for the next day, start the dishwasher and carry up my clean laundry to put away. This is a much better use of my time than my old habit of leaving the dishes until morning and tripping over my shoes on the way up the stairs.

Be Prepared

Therefore keep watch, because you do not know the day or the hour. (Matthew 25:13)

The ten virgins keeping watch for the bridegroom in Matthew 25 learned a valuable lesson in the importance of being prepared. The custom of that day was for the wedding party to wait for the bridegroom and follow him to the wedding feast. In this passage, Jesus shares a parable of Five foolish virgins who failed to bring enough oil to supply their lamps while they were waiting. They were forced to interrupt their vigil to get more oil and missed the arrival of the bridegroom. As a result, the Five foolish virgins were locked out of the feast.

Loosely applying the principle of this passage to shampoo and toothpaste instead of oil, I have cultivated the practice of keeping extras of frequently needed items on hand—like the linen closet supplies. Earlier we talked about organizing them once they were there. The concern of this section is the make sure they're there!

One day, I typed up a master list of the items I stock on this shelf. Now, I keep a pencil and a copy of this list posted inside the door. Our rule is: if you take something from this shelf, make a slash by the item. This way, I can grab the list to restock next time I make a trip to the discount store.

In the same closet is a shelf with small gifts for both children and adults. When my children are invited to a birthday party, they can select a gift from this shelf. I also keep gifts appropriate for adults—such as friends or teachers. But how do they get there? Well, I make it a practice to look for sale items to stock the gift shelf. It has been quite a money saver and it is a lifesaver when I have forgotten a special occasion!

Along these same lines, I maintain a greeting card organizer. Actually I have two different kinds and use both a lot. The first is a notebook with pockets for each month. On the outside of the pockets, I have listed the birthdays and anniversaries of family members and close friends. At the beginning of the year, I go to our local Christian bookstore and purchase greeting cards for the entire year. When I get home, I address and stamp all the birthday and anniversary cards and slip them into the appropriate pocket. I also note these dates on our family calendar. When a special occasion comes up, I just reach into my notebook, sign the card and slip it in the mail.

The other card organizer I use is a small file box. I have dividers to separate various kinds of cards: birthday, wedding, new baby, get well, sympathy, etc. I also restock these cards on my yearly shopping trip to the Christian bookstore so I am prepared when a special occasion arises.

The old boy scout motto, "Be prepared," holds a lot of truth. Just look what happened to the Five foolish virgins.

Free Your Mind

I will walk about in freedom,
   for I have sought out your precepts. (Psalm 119:45)

I know that God desires peace for me, but my mind used to operate on high speed the majority of the time, afraid I was going to forget what I needed to do, where I needed to go or what I needed to buy for the family. How could I find peace in the midst of all this mental chaos!

As I prayed about my overloaded mind, I began to recognize the value of using lists. And, as is generally the case, God got my attention through His Word, by prompting me to notice the little things around me. For example, I began to notice the numerous lists that are included in Scripture (the Ten Commandments, fruit of the Spirit, materials for the temple, etc.). I also began to notice women taking lists from their purses. And my husband was always making lists in the back of his planner. I also noticed teachers giving my children lists of supplies, directions, etc.

Well, I wasn't too keen on lists. Lists are not creative or spontaneous! Unfortunately, all this creativity and spontaneity in my life was driving me crazy. I was missing appointments, searching for phone numbers and going to the store for "just a few things" much too often. So, again, I reluctantly admitted my way was not best—or even good. I decided to follow God's example and began to make some lists of my own.

The first thing I did was to develop a phone list with emergency numbers and put it by each phone. This worked so well that I got the idea to type the most frequently used numbers (relatives, school, etc.) and put these by the phones also. I liked this idea so much that I transferred our entire address book to the computer and made little phone books for each phone. This little improvement saved so much time that it wasn't long before I began to change my mind about lists as the destroyers of creativity and spontaneity.

Next, I put my "master phone list" in a three-ring binder near the kitchen desk where I also keep the neighborhood, school and church directories. I use this master list to update any new phone numbers and addresses. When I write out Christmas cards, I use this book to update the computer file and print our new phone books. You can even use this file to print out a set of address labels, making the addressing of Christmas cards much easier.

Once I began to appreciate the wisdom of using lists, there was no stopping me! Here are a few ideas that have removed some of the clutter from my creative mind.

- I have a magnetic grocery list pad mounted on the refrigerator. When anyone in the family notices something we need from the grocery store, they jot it down on the list. No more forgetting the mustard or laundry detergent!

- I keep a list for errands and an "errand bag" hanging on a hook near the door. In this bag, I place library books that need to be returned, clothes that need to go to the dry cleaners, rolls of film that need developing, borrowed items to return, etc. I can just grab the list and bag on my way out the door.

- A daily checklist of my children's responsibilities and chores has dramatically cut the need to nag. I photocopied a whole stack of these chore checklists, and I put one for each child on the counter each morning. It's his or her responsibility to have a parent initial it when chores are completed—or face the predetermined consequences.

- Probably the most important list in our home is the family calendar. Our family calendar is actually a large desk-type calendar with pull-off sheets. You can generally purchase a calendar like this from an office supply store for just a few dollars. Each year, I glue several magnetic strips to the back of it and mount it on the refrigerator. You can even use the same magnetic strips year after year. My only complaint is that it's not very cute—but it works extremely well.

  My husband especially loves our calendar because it is large, easy to read and easy to use. One glance is all he needs to know what is on the schedule for that day or why there are fourteen little ballerinas coming up our front steps.

Busy Little Hands

Train a child in the way he should go,
  and when he is old he will not turn from it.
  (Proverbs 22:6)

Someday our children will be moving from our homes to their own. And those homes will need to be managed. I think one of the best things we can do as parents is to train our children to care for themselves and their things at a very young age.

> *Lazy hands make a man poor [or his mother's sore!].*
> (10:4)

I have found that if you take the time to train children to care for their things and help with household chores, you will reap great rewards. Be firm and consistent. The checklists described earlier are a great help and seriously cut down nagging.

This training goes much more smoothly if I try to make it easy for my children to care for their own things. For example, I have developed a system for laundry that requires personal responsibility, not mine—theirs.

I try to do laundry each day and will wash all of the dirty clothes that are placed in the laundry chute from the previous day. This requires two to three loads per day for our family of Five who live at home. Clean clothing not hung on the rack in the laundry room is folded directly into baskets labeled with the name of each family member. The children are responsible each evening for putting away their clean laundry and returning the laundry basket and empty hangers to the laundry room. Again, I use the checklist as a reminder.

Here are some other tips you might find useful for helping your children become true helpers:

- For the older children, hang most of the clothing. The younger ones find it easier to keep clothing folded in drawers.
- Plastic bins and shelves seem to work well to corral toys. For younger children, you might attach a pic-

ture of the toy (Barbies, cars, Legos, etc.) to the bin to help them put things away properly. The key to maintaining order with toys is to not have too many. Rotate toys if you must, but do something to drastically cut down on the number.

- Install hooks near the door for backpacks, etc. Make sure they are low enough for little ones. You may want to put hooks inside the closet door for younger children or install an over-the-door rack for older kids.

    My pastor came up with a great idea for his three boys. He built little locker-like cubbies in the garage near the door for each son. There are hooks for coats, backpacks and sports bags, a place for shoes and boots and an upper shelf for hats and gloves. And to think he can preach a great sermon too!

- I keep a tub for shoes right inside the door. The entire family makes a practice of kicking their shoes into this tub as they come in the house. Each evening, my youngest daughter is responsible for putting away all the shoes from the tub.

- Baskets seem to work best for videotapes, CDs and video games. Kids are much more likely to toss something in a basket than line it up in a drawer or cabinet.

- We have a rack in our garage designed for sports equipment. It's mounted on the wall and works wonderfully! Check discount, hardware or a home specialty stores for this. You might also find a sports rack in some mail-order catalogs. I also noticed that a lot of soccer balls, etc., were being left in the backyard. I put a hinged and rain- proofed plastic chest on the porch to make it easy to keep equipment handy and organized.

- Require that hobbies, collections, musical instruments, music stands, etc., be kept in children's own rooms.
- I recycle Five-gallon buckets as snack buckets. I just dump in sealed packages of granola bars, chips and other kid-friendly snacks. This makes it easy to grab a quick after-school snack or put together a cold lunch.
- As mentioned in a previous chapter, a hanging shoe bag is a wonderful organizer for hats, gloves and scarves. This is much better than digging through a drawer or closet that seems to devour one glove from each pair.
- And last, but not least, my favorite tip. It came from my husband. Each child has a pair of towels in a different color with his or her name monogrammed on it. No more guessing who left the towel on the floor!

Walk Wisely

It is very important to remember that God cares about how we spend our time. I think we show our love and devotion for Him by being good stewards of our days. If you struggle in this area, confess your weakness to God. You can depend on Him to encourage, teach and strengthen you. He is Almighty God, and He loves to bless His children!

The LORD is my strength and my song. (Exodus 15:2)

Going Deeper

1. What obstacles do you encounter when it comes to managing your time effectively?

2. Keep a detailed diary of your activities for an entire day (a week is better). Did you find any surprises? Where do you spend most of your time?

3. Read Haggai 1:5-6. Why do we often find ourselves "[planting] much, but [harvesting] little"?

4. Read Ephesians 5:15-16. How can clarifying our mission and goals as a family help to make the most of our time?

5. Use a Bible concordance to locate and read all references to "sluggard" in the book of Proverbs. Why do you think God places so much emphasis on rising early? How would this habit benefit you? What changes can you make to become a morning person?

6. Read Acts 5:38. Why is it important to ask God to guide our daily to-do list? What does this act of submission communicate to God? How might this impact our day?

7. Read Proverbs 14:1. In what way can procrastination "tear our house down"? What are the benefits of breaking this habit? What can you do today to begin breaking the habit of procrastination?

8. What time-saving systems or methods have you employed in your home?
9. Do you use lists? If so, what kind and how have they helped you?
10. Read Proverbs 10:4 and 22:6. Why is it crucial that we take the time to train our children to share in household responsibilities and care for their possessions? Share with your group systems and strategies that have worked well in your home.

CHAPTER SIX

The
Occasional
Cook

Go to the ant, you sluggard;
consider its ways and be wise! . . .
it stores its provisions in summer
and gathers its food at harvest.
(Proverbs 6:6, 8)

The Occasional Cook

Ask any mother where she spends the most amount of time and she'll probably include in her answer the kitchen, the car and the grocery store. That's why developing a system that streamlines food preparation—from purchase to the table—is a crucial step in efficient home management. I know from personal experience that this will save you a great amount of time, but more importantly, it will strengthen your family life.

As I shared earlier, when I finally relinquished control of my home to God, He began to teach me His ways. "The Occasional Cook" is one of the firstfruits that came from being connected to the Vine.

A Pleasing Aroma

God calls the smell of cooking food "an aroma pleasing to me" (Numbers 28:2). In the New Testament, some of Jesus' most powerful teachings were preceded or followed by food. Even when teaching about prayer, Jesus instructed us to ask God for our daily bread. This sharing of daily bread not only meets a physical need, but it also allows families precious time to reconnect and build relationships.

Yet surveys reveal some frightening facts about our culture:

- forty percent of families today do not eat together
- one in ten meals is eaten in the car. (Source: *Omaha World Herald*, March, 1997)

It doesn't take a scholar to conclude that mealtimes are not meeting the emotional needs of many families nor doing a good job of meeting the physical needs of good health and nutrition. These statistics are truly heart-breaking when I think about the impact this lifestyle is having on children who have a vital need for nurturing and stability, not to mention the emotional and financial stress it causes parents.

Surveys of parents also tell us that they are spending a major portion of their time and budget grocery shopping. Many also list grocery shopping as one of their least desirable household chores. Do you see yourself and your family in these statistics? I certainly did.

A Reluctant Ant

"The Occasional Cook" follows the premise of the tale of the industrious ant who works hard to store food for the winter while the grasshopper plays in the sun. You know who will end up enjoying evenings by the fire while the other is knocking at the door to the anthill. I used to be an unhappy grasshopper (without even knowing it) but, for the last several years, I have found myself in the role of industrious ant. Let me tell you what am I really talking about.

Basically, "The Occasional Cook" is a system where you spend about a day and a half every six weeks preparing meals for the freezer. This allows you to pretty much cross "prepare dinner" from your daily to-do list. I have been doing this for several years and have become a true believer in its effectiveness.

"The Occasional Cook" works well for people who absolutely love to cook and for those who absolutely hate to cook. How can this be? Let me explain.

Sometimes I love to cook. That's probably why I was initially attracted to the idea of preparing and freezing meals in advance. A full day in the kitchen didn't intimidate me. In fact, I even looked forward to it as a kind of a mini-vacation from the chaos of the rest of my house.

However, after cooking all day for the first time, I was very, very tired. In fact, I thought I might have truly fallen off the proverbial deep end this time. I never wanted to see another onion for the rest of my days much less sauté one.

Nevertheless, after recovering from my cooking hangover, I began to feel a real sense of peace and accomplishment. I found myself staring in my freezer and marveling that I had thirty-six meals ready to go! I called my husband and children to the garage to look in the freezer and marvel with me. (This didn't go over as well as I hoped.) They were quite complimentary, but they certainly couldn't grasp the inexpressible joy I felt when I realized I probably would not have to cook another meal for at least six weeks.

As time went on, I found ways to streamline my cooking day and incorporate my own recipes. I began to include dinners for celebrations (birthdays, holidays, etc.) as well as extras like side dishes, desserts, cookies or muffins. It all depended on my mood and energy level.

Through the years, I have fine-tuned the method to meet my needs and the needs of my family. (For example, we now follow a fairly low-fat diet, so most of my recipes reflect this change in lifestyle.) Those of you with children know that as your children grow their needs and schedules are constantly changing. This brings me to my second point.

There are times in my life that I absolutely hate to cook. Between volunteer activities, running my consulting business and shuttling children all over town, I am often too busy to shop, cook and (heaven forbid) clean up the kitchen.

It used to be that during these times when my mind was too full to handle another thing, guilt would descend like a dark cloud. I could hear the frustration in my husband's voice when I would tell him I had been too busy to get around to dinner as he said, "Don't worry about it. I can pick up another pizza. Oh, I didn't mean another. . . ." Never mind what all those pizzas and trips through drive-thru windows did to our budget—and to our waistlines.

Today, those times when I used to feel guilty because I couldn't get around to dinner have been virtually eliminated. Instead, when I have a busy day, dinner is one thing I don't even have to think about. It's already done! I just take a meal from the freezer and spend a few seconds thinking about what to serve with it (if anything). I might even toss some ingredients in my breadmaker and set the timer so a fresh loaf of bread is ready at 6 p.m.

My mind is clear and definitely free of guilt. When I walk through the door after a long day, dinner is ready to go and the house smells like freshly baked bread. This is a much better start to the evening than french fries in the car. . . . And, as a family, we can sit down together and talk for a few minutes before we go our separate ways in the evening. My husband and I might even linger over a cup of coffee while the kids load the dishwasher. (And they don't complain too loudly because there are few, if any, pots and pans to clean up.)

A Pot Full o' Ministry Opportunities

Very quickly I began to see this cooking system as much more than a way to cut down on my workload at home. I truly believe it is a God-given ministry to my husband, children and others.

God gave me a wonderful man to share my life, and He also gave me a clear set of instructions to keep our marriage on a victorious path. I am very blessed that my husband takes very seriously his responsibility to provide for our family. I think one of the ways I can honor him for this and show my appreciation is to try to make our home a haven from the pressures of the world. A nice meal to begin our evening is a great start. We have also realized significant savings in our grocery budget. (This always goes over well with husbands!)

The same is true for my children, another focus of ministry. "The Occasional Cook" has brought order to what used to be a chaotic time of day for us. It allows me to slow down and take time with my children after school. I can make sure homework is getting done, go over spelling words with them and tell them that I adore each one of them, but more importantly, so does their Creator.

> *Better a dry crust with peace and quiet*
> *than a house full of feasting, with strife.*
> (Proverbs 17:1)

Through my well-stocked freezer, I have also been able to reach out to others. I always have a meal ready for a sick friend or family in need, or I may use a meal to show appreciation to special teachers or a dear friend.

My meals have also allowed me to witness to strangers. The following story is a powerful example of how God can work, if we are prepared and willing to take the opportunity He gives us. God can use seemingly insignificant things to change lives, and it's important for us to be ready to act when He calls us.

A few years ago, a woman from Florida visited a Bible study I attend. She shared with our group that she had come to visit her parents. While here, her brother became suddenly and seriously ill. Sadly, he died the next day. When I found out about it, I offered to bring a meal to her family that evening. She said that would meet a great need since the family was still in a state of shock. I agreed to drop dinner by in a couple of hours and asked how many I should cook for. Her answer was "about twenty-four people." I gulped and said I would see her soon.

Instead of going through my fried chicken coupons (a real temptation), I looked in the freezer. I spied three containers of homemade spaghetti sauce and began thawing them in the microwave. Next, I put some Italian bread mix in my breadmaker, threw together a salad (salad in a bag is such a blessing!) and began boiling pasta. While the bread baked, I had time to write a note of support and encouragement to the family. I delivered the food to a grieving group of people (many who were not Christians) that wondered what would motivate a complete stranger to prepare dinner for them. My card provided the answer. In showing love to them, I was showing my love for God (Matthew 25:34-40).

About a month later, I received a beautiful note from the woman in Florida. She wanted me to know that my spaghetti dinner had been a very powerful witness to her family. She said, "You can't know how your outpouring of love to complete strangers, with apparently nothing to gain, witnessed to my family, many of whom are unbelievers. They just couldn't understand why you would go to all that trouble for them. I had an opportunity to share Jesus with them when they saw how much He meant in your life. You brought much more than food to our family." And to think this resulted from less than an hour of my time that day. God truly works in wonderful ways!

When we are obedient to God's prompting in our lives, He blesses us richly. It is hard to believe all the wonderful things that have resulted from the occasional cooking plan. It has freed up time to do many things I truly enjoy like spending the afternoon over tea with a friend or reading a good book or going out to dinner with my husband while the kids eat a special "kids' dinner" I've tucked away in the freezer for them. Just knowing that making good use of my time honors God brings me a deep sense of peace and joy.

"The Occasional Cook" System

In the following pages, I will outline the basic method for this system (which, as you've probably guessed by now, is also a cookbook I've compiled). It's important to remember that the system is designed to fit the individual needs of the cook who is using it. As you work with it, you will find yourself adapting it in numerous ways. That's the idea. For example, you may follow the system as written and complete all of your meals in a day. Or, you may spread the work out over two or three afternoons. I have even used the system to prepare Christmas cookies or breakfast entrees.

Be creative!

You will also find that the first time you cook will probably take a very long time. You may get very tired. The evening I finished cooking for the first time, I was certain nothing was worth the effort I had expended that day. But I changed my mind after just a few evenings of reaping the rewards of my hard work (and sore back).

If you enjoy the system, you might want to add side dishes or breakfast dishes to your plan. I sometimes make cookie dough and freeze it in long rolls that are ready to slice and bake. (I really feel like June Cleaver when my kids can enjoy fresh-baked cookies when they come home from school. Maybe I should invest in some pearls.)

You may also choose to simplify the system with easy recipes and convenience foods which allow you to put together twenty to thirty meals in one afternoon. The key is to take the time at the start to learn the system and experiment until it works for you.

Planning

Step 1: The first step is to gather together several recipes for main entrees that you enjoy. As you will see from the few recipes I have included at the back of this book, I like to use a basic recipe (stew, chili, etc.) and vary it with seasonings or use it several different ways. Or I may double or triple a family favorite. Remember, this is not the time to be too adventurous. For the first few times you cook, stick to family favorites you are familiar preparing.

Try to select a mixture of dishes (chicken, beef, pork, fish, vegetarian, bean, cheese, egg). You will also want to vary the method of preparation somewhat. You don't want to end up with all casseroles. For example, you may want to include:

- meats that may be prepared on the grill or broiler (marinated chicken, shish kabobs)
- comfort foods (meatloaf, roast beef, chicken with gravy)
- stews or soups (beef stroganoff, chili, chicken soup, lentil or bean soup)
- casseroles or layered dishes (chicken divan, taco casserole, chicken enchiladas)
- sandwiches (sloppy joes, French dip, BBQ chicken sandwiches)
- pasta dishes (one or two sauces that can be used in a variety of ways)
- brunch dishes (quiche, egg casserole)
- "kid meals" (make-your-own pizzas, macaroni and cheese casserole, chicken nuggets)

I almost always include a large pot of pasta sauce (usually marinara), soup (made from leftover vegetables and meat), a large beef roast (cooked in the crockpot) and marinated chicken and/or fish.

Be sure to select meals that fit into your lifestyle and dietary guidelines. If you eat a low-fat diet, select recipes that meet these requirements. Many favorite recipes can be modified with the variety of low-fat and fat-free products available today. For example, a quiche or egg casserole can be made using an egg-product substitute and low-fat cheese. Also, many recipes that call for frying can be prepared with very little oil in a non-stick pan or cooked in the oven.

I almost always include one new recipe (maybe two). When I serve it, the family is encouraged to make an honest assessment by voting thumbs up, thumbs down or so-so. That is an easy way to decide what meals to include in the future.

A warning! Be careful about experimenting too much with new recipes or substitutions if you are doubling or tripling a recipe. You don't want to end up with three dishes your family won't eat! If you are not sure about a recipe, my suggestion is to try one batch first and see how it freezes. If it is a success, next cooking day you may decide to double, triple or even quadruple it.

Step 2: After you have selected your recipes and determined how many of each you will prepare, make a list of the ingredients you need for each recipe. Remember to multiply each ingredient by the number of meals you plan to make with it. Then combine common ingredients onto a master list. For example, I often find I have twenty cups of onions on my list.

I have found it easier to make a copy of each recipe, three hole punch it and slip it into a binder. This is especially helpful when I plan to double or triple a recipe. I am able to calculate the ingredients for the number of meals and write the new proportions right on the copy in the binder. This system also frees me from having to flip through a variety of cookbooks or my recipe file on cooking day.

Step 3: Check your pantry for the ingredients on your master list that you may have on hand. Take dry goods out of the pantry and place them in a bag or on a counter. It is extremely important to actually check your pantry for the ingredients. I know how important this is from experience. I have been certain that I had an ingredient on hand, but in the middle of cooking day could not locate it or found an empty box. This really throws off the entire process (and aggravates my husband, who usually runs to the store for me).

Step 4: Next, decide how you will package and freeze each meal. List the needed packaging materials or containers for each meal in your notebook and put them on the counter. Add anything you need to buy to your grocery list.

I use a lot of freezer bags (quart, gallon and two-gallon sizes) because they take up less space. For example, I freeze meatloaf flat in a gallon bag; I put marinade in a bag and toss in frozen chicken breasts, and I use bags for sliced meat and gravy, casseroles (not layered), hamburger patties, cheese or bread crumbs for toppings, etc. Two-gallon bags can hold several smaller bags for one meal. For example, you can put sloppy joes in one bag, buns in another and package both in one two-gallon bag. Bags work well because you can remove air and preserve the quality of the contents.

I freeze layered casseroles or dishes that are finished in the oven in baking dishes. It is a good idea to choose microwave-proof glass or ceramic dishes in case you need to thaw or heat something quickly. I suggest putting pasta sauces and soups in plastic containers to prevent leakage. The key to preserving quality is to fit the container to the amount of food. Try to leave very little air space (1/4"). Have a good permanent marking pen available to label and date the containers.

Step 5: The next step is to make a grocery list. Be sure to include all ingredients as well as packaging supplies on your list. I like to organize the list by store (if I plan to use more than one) and aisle, if possible. This cuts down on shopping time and leaves less possibility for forgetting an ingredient.

While you're at it, why not buy yourself something special to eat for lunch on your cooking day?

Step 6: Determine the best order to assemble and/or cook recipes, and write down a game plan to guide you through your cooking day. The first tasks on my plan include chopping, slicing, crushing, shredding and browning all ingredients. Your plan should include amounts to prepare such as "chop twenty cups of onions," or "shred one pound of cheese." Next, I plan to assemble the slow cooking items so they can simmer while I work on other meals. Then, I list meals to assemble by categories (ground beef, marinated dishes, etc.). Finally, I plan on packaging slow-simmering dishes that have cooled.

This game plan is very important on cooking day. The more you cook, the easier it will be to put together a plan. I have included a sample plan and a few of my favorite recipes at the back of this book.

The Day Before

Step 7: The next step is to go shopping and purchase everything on your list. I usually shop at three stores. First, I stop at a warehouse store for bulk items such as frozen chicken breasts, large roasts, large cans of vegetables (tomatoes, etc.), dry beans, rice and some produce items (if quality looks good). I sometimes find good deals on freezer bags or plastic containers here too.

Next, I stop at a "no frills" type store that offers discount prices in return for very little ambiance and service. This is where I purchase the remainder of my canned goods, frozen vegetables and dairy products as well as most of my meat and produce (depending on quality).

I may have a few specialty items on my list that I buy from my regular full-service grocery store. This is a good place to pick up bakery and deli items you may need. Also, the butcher is usually more willing to cut and slice meat a certain way if you request it.

I have found that shopping at more than one store is the best way to save money, but sometimes I just don't have the time to do it. Do what fits best with your lifestyle and budget. Remember, this system is designed to save you time, not monopolize it.

Step 8: As soon as you get home, unload your groceries. I unload right to my kitchen table so the ingredients are readily accessible, unless of course the food needs to be refrigerated or frozen. Be sure to defrost what needs to be defrosted in time for your cooking day.

Next, set out all the packaging materials (ziplock bags, freezer containers, etc.) you will need for the recipes you have selected. This is a good time to pull out necessary pans, food processors, blenders, etc. The goal is to be ready to cook as soon as you reach the kitchen. I even get my morning coffee ready to brew.

Step 9: I usually do a little precooking the evening before cooking day. This helps me get started right away in the morning and makes the day run much more smoothly.

For instance, I boil, skin and bone all of my chickens so the meat is ready for recipes. Then, I put the broth in the refrigerator to chill. In the morning, I skim the fat from the top of the broth and use it for soup. (With some leftover chicken and vegetables, this makes a great soup.)

I also put a roast in the crockpot and turn it on low before I go to bed. In the morning, the meat is tender and juicy, ready to cool and package. This also frees my crockpot for other uses during the day. (I picked up a second crockpot at a garage sale, and it has really helped on cooking day. It is nice to put spaghetti sauce, soup or stew in it and let it simmer without worrying about burning it.) Also, don't forget to soak any dry beans you might be using.

Step 10: Get a good night's sleep.

Cooking Day

Step 11: Fill one side of your sink with warm soapy water. You will need to wash dishes as you cook throughout the day. This will keep the kitchen in order, and there will be less chance of confusion and/or contamination. Put on an apron, and pull out your game plan.

Step 12: The first list of tasks on your plan should include chopping, shredding, dicing, crushing, etc. I have found that my food processor works very well for this. Keep chopped onions in a covered container in water. You can make great homemade bread crumbs from leftover bread using your food processor.

I put all of my scraps of vegetables (including skins, tops, peelings, etc.), as well as bones and meat trimmings, in a crockpot turned on low. With some water, a few spices and perhaps a can of tomatoes, this makes a wonderful stock for soup or sauces. At the end of the day, strain the broth, add leftover vegetables and meat and you have a great soup. If you don't need the stock right away, freeze it in small containers.

Step 13: Next, I start a large pot of spaghetti sauce and/or soup or stew simmering. It's nice to get slow-cooking dishes or sauces going early so they will be cool enough to package at the end of the day. (Note: Sometimes I prepare such dishes the day before my cooking day to save time assembling dishes.)

Step 14: Keep a close eye on your game plan. You should be at the point of assembling other recipes, some of which are cooked, partially cooked or ready-to-cook. (Remember to do the cooked dishes first so they have time to cool before packaging. Marinated dishes or casseroles that aren't cooked can be done later.)

Step 15: Package each dish after it has cooled. Be sure to label all packages with the name of the dish and the date. You may also want to put baking or cooking instructions for some dishes on the package.

Step 16: Make an inventory list of the meals you have assembled. I post this list on the inside of the cupboard door and cross out meals as they are used.

Step 17: Go out to dinner! You definitely deserve a break.

Be sure to check out page 193 for some of my favorite recipes and page 198 for a sample "game plan" for using "The Occasional Cook" system.

Going Deeper

1. What challenges do you face when it comes to planning and preparing an evening meal for your family?
2. Statistics indicate that forty percent of families do not eat dinner together, and one in ten meals is eaten in the car. What do you think are the reasons for this trend? What impact do you think this is having on families?
3. Read Haggai 1:6. For the next week, keep a tally of the amount of money spent on meals away from home (fast food, restaurants, school lunches, etc.). Are there any changes you would like to make to improve nutrition and make better use of the resources God has given you?
3. Read John 6:5-13. Why do you think Jesus wanted to share a meal with those He was teaching? How can we apply this to our own children?
4. What are the emotional benefits of regularly sharing an evening meal with your family?
5. Read Proverbs 17:1. In what ways might planning and preparing meals in advance have a positive impact on your late afternoon/early evenings?
6. Has someone ever brought a meal to you? How did this act of kindness make you feel? Have you ever reached out to another person with a meal? What was their response? Why is this act of kindness such a powerful witness?
7. Go through your recipe file and select three to Five recipes that would freeze well to share with your group.

CHAPTER SEVEN

Like a White Tornado!

He stilled the storm to a whisper. (Psalm 107:29)

Like a White Tornado!

Although I don't remember the product, I'll never forget the commercial. A "white tornado" would sweep into a home leaving sparkling surfaces and a grateful homemaker in its wake. Just as I once thought Alice might be a reality in my life someday, I also harbored a secret desire for a white tornado to rescue me from the drudgery of cleaning. Unfortunately, the only tornadoes that have swept through my house were wearing muddy tennis shoes . . . all the way up the stairs . . . on beige carpeting.

But even in the midst of a storm, God doesn't forget about us. I found I could depend on Him to guide and strengthen me even when it came to cleaning house!

Talk to the Pros

A wise man listens to advice. (Proverbs 12:15)

It was not too difficult for me to face up to the fact that cleaning was not one of my strengths. I did not like it, and besides, I was not good at it. In fact, my husband called me "dangerous." More than once, in my zeal to finish cleaning as quickly as possible, I mixed cleaners together that produced toxic fumes, once almost sending me to the emergency room.

One day, I decided to tackle the ceramic tile in the shower with a mixture of ammonia and chlorine bleach. Fortunately, John heard me coughing and quickly threw open windows all over the house. Without his quick thinking, I might have been a cleaning casualty. As you can see, I definitely needed help in this area.

Since "Alice" was a distant dream, I sought the advice of the pros, real janitors, who used real products, not the sissy stuff they sold to housewives at the grocery store. From the experts at the janitorial supply store, I discovered I had been buying several products that were actually doing more damage to my home than good. These pros explained what products and tools I needed and how to use them correctly—and safely. Armed with the right equipment, I began to feel a little like a white tornado myself!

Choose Your Weapons

I spent a couple hours at the janitorial supply store the first time I visited. (You can find listings for these stores in the Yellow Pages. Most will sell to the general public.) I browsed for a while by myself, realizing I had no idea what the labels meant and finally asked for help.

I wanted to know which was the best product for each job. To my surprise, I found that one chemical was best for just about everything. It's called "neutral cleaner" or all-purpose neutral cleaner/degreaser. I also bought a specialty cleaner for glass and mirrors as well as disinfectant. The clerk suggested I buy some treated dust rags and a dust mop. (It turned out to be great!) I spent much less money than I had anticipated and I'm using the same tools several years later.

Most of the products come in concentrated form. Although you need to take an extra minute to mix them with water in a spray bottle, the concentrates last for a long time. In fact, I only have to buy cleaners once every two or three years.

The following is my suggested shopping list for the janitorial supply store. However, be sure to ask the sales staff for products to fit your cleaning needs.

- Neutral Cleaner/Degreaser Concentrate (can be used on most surfaces, including floors)
- Glass Cleaner Concentrate (for glass and mirrors)
- Disinfectant Concentrate (kills germs in the kitchen and bathroom)
- Spray bottles (to mix cleaners)
- Disposable dust rags
- Static duster (optional—great for fans, shelves, woodwork, etc.)
- Large industrial dust mop (optional—great on all floors including vinyl, wood or tile)
- Professional squeegee (a "must" for cleaning windows)
- Specialty products such as pumice (to remove hard water rings in the toilet bowl), metal polish, furniture wax, products to remove hard water and mildew.

Once you have purchased and mixed your cleaners, locate a large bucket or other container to hold all of your supplies. (I recycled an empty Five-gallon bucket for this purpose.) I also put in a roll of paper towels, a few cleaning rags and a scrubber sponge. (I still like to use powdered cleanser for tough jobs and the toilet bowls, so I put a can of this in my bucket also.)

Clutter Control

> I have learned that man can live profoundly without masses of things.
>
> —Admiral Byrd, from his journal
> during an Arctic expedition

Clutter is the single biggest barrier to cleaning your home efficiently. Therefore, I encourage you to decorate as simply as possible. A table or countertop with numerous knickknacks to move takes three times as long to clean. God (I think) has a much better use for my time than the constant removing, dusting and replacing of an excessive number of decorative items.

By now, other clutter such as newspapers, mail, shoes, etc., should be of minimal concern if you have followed the advice in previous chapters. If not, before you begin cleaning, I suggest grabbing a large laundry basket and making a quick sweep around the room to pick up anything that doesn't belong. Put the contents of the laundry basket in its proper place when you have finished cleaning.

Speed Cleaning

My days are swifter than a weaver's shuttle. (Job 7:6)

There are some people who say they genuinely like to clean and even feel that housecleaning is good for the soul. Unfortunately, I'm not one of them—I prefer restoring my spirit in other ways. Therefore, my goal is to clean as quickly and efficiently as possible and then spend the time I've saved enjoying the results. In fact, I often reward myself for cleaning the bathroom with a bubble bath in my sparkling tub.

Cleaning Principle #1: Clean from top to bottom. Apart from removing clutter, there are just two principles to cleaning quickly and efficiently. The first is to clean from top to bottom. Start with your static duster to remove cobwebs from things like ceiling fans and bookshelves. Work your way down and around the room sweeping crumbs, dust, etc., to the floor.

Cleaning Principles #2: Give the cleaning products time to work. The second principle to cleaning efficiently is to give the products time to work. This is especially important in kitchens and baths where you need to remove dried-on food, grease or hard-water spots. Here are some tips on how to clean a bathroom in under ten minutes:

- Clear all surfaces and spray everything (counters, sinks, toilet, tub, shower) except the mirror with neutral cleaner/disinfectant.
- While the cleaner works, spray the mirror with glass cleaner and wipe with paper towels.
- Wipe down the sink with a damp sponge or rag.
- Use paper towels to dry and polish the sink counter and chrome.
- Sprinkle inside of toilet with powdered cleanser or toilet cleaner. Swish with rag or brush. Use pumice to remove hard water rings.
- Use a damp rag or sponge to wipe down the toilet and tank.

- Use scrubber sponge to clean the tub and shower. Rinse. Some people have had great results with spray-on products that do the same thing. As a matter of fact, you can probably avoid having to clean this area at all by using a squeegee or towel to wipe down the shower.
- Run a damp paper towel over the floor to pick up debris.
- Spray floor, and wipe up with damp rag.

All done!

The same principles may be applied in the other "wet" rooms: clean from top to bottom and give the products time to work.

Here's my checklist for the kitchen:

- Clear counters in kitchen, thoroughly spray surfaces and appliances with neutral cleaner/disinfectant. Allow cleaner to work for a couple of minutes, then wipe clean.
- You may need to use a scrubber sponge on the stove and in the microwave. (A neat trick is to boil a bowl of water in the microwave to loosen the "gunk" stuck to the sides.)
- If necessary, wipe down cabinets, dining table and chairs with neutral cleaner.
- Use cleanser to scrub the sink.
- Sweep up debris from floor and mop or wash using a solution of vinegar and water.

The same principles work for the living areas.

- Move around the room, dusting from top to bottom with a treated dust cloth and static duster.

Don't forget windowsills, ceiling fans, bookshelves
and picture frames.

- Use a paper towel dampened with window cleaner
to clean and shine television screens and pictures.
- Run the vacuum over the carpeting. To keep upholstered pieces looking fresh, vacuum occasionally.

Just like a white tornado!

Mountains and Molehills

I used to be of the mind-set that the only time I should
clean was during the time I set aside to "really clean."
Therefore, if it wasn't my "cleaning day," I would ignore
little messes which promptly turned into big messes.
Through the years, however, I've found that if I take care of
the little messes right away, I can "really clean" less often.

For example, I now spot-clean the kitchen floor and
carpeting instead of waiting to clean or vacuum the entire area. I've found that picking up lint from the stairs or
using a whisk broom to brush off debris means I have to
vacuum less often. If I keep up with little smudges on
windows, they look clean longer.

Disinfectant wipes are available to help keep up the
bathroom between cleanings. There's no getting around
it: dealing with a little mess right away is much easier
than tackling the whole thing a few days later.

A Stitch in Time

How you accomplish cleaning your home depends on
your lifestyle and your personality. For example, a busy

lifestyle may not allow you to have your whole house clean at once. Instead, you might clean one or two rooms in a day. Some people divide cleaning up by floors, doing the upstairs one morning and the main floor another day.

My favorite way to clean is to get help from my family. We divide up all the cleaning chores, write them on slips of paper and ask everyone to draw one. We each get to work, and when finished, enjoy a reward together. Two keys to making this system work is to determine a reasonable time limit for the tasks to be completed and a reasonable standard of quality.

My point in all this is to encourage you to be creative and ask God for the wisdom to discern the best way to get this often unpleasant, but very necessary, job done.

Calm in the Storm

By now, I hope you are all ready to put out the storm warning, announcing the arrival of the "white tornado." Again, remember to let God guide you. He'll show you His way and His path.

> *Show me your ways, O LORD,*
>   *teach me your paths;*
> *guide me in your truth and teach me,*
>   *for you are God my Savior.* (Psalm 25:4-5)

Going Deeper

1. Read Isaiah 38:14. Is this your experience when you are faced with the task of cleaning your home?

2. What are your "pet" cleaning problems?
3. Read Proverbs 12:15. Where can you find the pros in your area? Have you ever used professional cleaning products? What were the results?
4. What slows down your ability to clean your home quickly and easily? What changes do you need to make?
5. List the principles of speed cleaning. Share other cleaning methods and strategies that you have used successfully to clean your home.
6. Read Psalm 107:29. Can you trust God to calm the storm in your home?

CHAPTER EIGHT

June's Touch

Her children arise and call her blessed;
her husband also, and he praises her.
(Proverbs 31:28)

June's Touch

Wouldn't it be soothing to live in a home that looked like the Cleaver household? No shoes littering the front hall. Dishes done. Windows sparkling. Fresh flowers gracing the dinner table. Viewers could almost smell the aroma of June's freshly baked cookies right through the television screen.

"Television" is the operative word here. Just like the air-brushed and liposuctioned actresses we see in movies and on television today, the Cleaver household was not reality. (I bet the windows of the set didn't even have glass in them! No wonder they always looked so clean!) Regardless, most of us easily fall into the trap of comparing ourselves with the images we see in the media. As we watch Martha Stewart whip up gorgeous fall table arrangements from sticks and fallen leaves after creating a sumptuous dinner for ten—all in the span of thirty minutes—it's easy to forget she has 100 people (probably a slight exaggeration) working behind the scenes to inspire and assist her.

If you've come to this point in the book, you know that I am not Martha Stewart, nor will I ever be. (In fact, I still can't figure out how to use my hot glue gun without getting third-degree burns.) However, as I've grown in my relationship with God, seeking to be obedient to His call to minister to my family, I've discovered some simple ways to bring a bit of what I refer to as "June's Touch" to life in our home.

Bring Nature Indoors

Now the LORD God had planted a garden in the east, in Eden; and there he put the man he had formed. And the LORD God made all kinds of trees grow out of the ground—trees that were pleasing to the eye and good for food. (Genesis 2:8-9)

I don't think it was a coincidence that God placed man in a garden at creation. What better way to be introduced to life than with the soothing sights and smells of a garden! And what a wonderful gift from our Creator! When we bring the natural beauty of flowers and plants indoors, our home also takes on a soothing quality and lifts our spirits.

For many years, I was a "silk flower person" for the simple fact that I seemed to kill just about any plant I came in contact with. Occasionally, I would splurge and buy a bouquet of fresh flowers from the grocery store. It was always sad when the blooms faded and I had to toss them out. But fresh flowers seemed to be an extravagance.

One morning, while visiting our local farmer's market, I impulsively purchased a bouquet from a flower vendor and was overcome with delight when she presented me with two huge bouquets (a two-for-one sale) that barely fit in the car with my other purchases. At home, I pulled out every vase I could find and ended up with fresh flowers in almost every room, including the bathroom. What a joy their beauty brought to my spirit! I was hooked!

However, since purchasing fresh flowers for every room on a regular basis was not in our budget, I reluctantly decided to try to develop a green thumb so I could grow my own. With the advice of friends and a jar of cosmos seeds from Uncle Ralph, I planted my first flower garden by scattering the seeds on the ground and then trampling over them for a few minutes. Much to my surprise, the seeds produced a gorgeous profusion of flowers that graced our home all summer long. I have to admit, I did feel a bit like Martha Stewart as I went out to the garden with my basket to snip flowers for the dinner table. I even considered buying a straw hat!

Today, I grow a cutting garden from both seeds and perennials so that I have a ready supply of blooms from early spring to late fall. Some of my favorites are cosmos, daisies, coreopsis, zinnias, lilac, mums, lavender and astilbe. Although some of the plants in my garden are annuals, they often self-seed and surprise me by sprouting the next spring.

We have also planted a flowering crab tree and several flowering bushes in our yard. It is wonderful to usher in spring by bringing a few blooming branches in the house. Many of the branches from flowering trees or bushes can also be "forced" to bloom in winter by bringing them indoors, placing them in a vase with fresh water and waiting patiently for the buds to open.

Spring and summer aren't the only times to enjoy nature indoors. In the fall, I may snip branches from trees or bushes in the yard which have turned a vibrant shade of red or yellow. Even in the dead of our Nebraska winter, my neighbors often see me climbing the hill behind our home in my old snow boots to snip pine boughs from the evergreen trees. I make a winter bouquet by placing them in water with some trimmings from plants that have winter berries. The scent of pine that fills the house is an added bonus.

Several years ago, I decided to put some perennial herbs in my garden—sage, tarragon, oregano and mint. In addition to cooking, I use the herbs to garnish dishes, flavor tea and serve as fragrant greenery in bouquets. Edible flowers like nasturtiums can also be used to spice up a green salad. (I must admit, my children were a little wary about eating flowers at first, but now they love to pop them in their mouths just to impress their friends.)

A word of caution is in order. Although a garden is wonderful, don't allow it to become an undue burden on you or your family. A wise friend passed on some wonderful advice one day as I lamented about the weeding and pruning I needed to do in the garden. She said, "Cyndy, remember, your garden is for your enjoyment, not to make you a slave to it." What freedom those few words gave me. I have since decided to plant mostly wildflowers or perennials because they require a minimum of care. In fact, one year when the weeds became particularly bad in the garden, I quipped to friends that I was allowing the prairie to regenerate!

So whether you garden in a pot or a plot, I want to encourage you to capture the beauty of the changing seasons by bringing nature into your home all year long. And give thanks to our Creator for this wonderful blessing.

Create a Cozy Environment

Come with me . . . to a quiet place and get some rest.
(Mark 6:31)

Nothing draws a family together like a cozy room and a bowl of popcorn. I think every family should have a room where you can put your feet up, and it doesn't really matter if a little popcorn falls between the cushions.

This room, in our home, is the family room which is adjacent to the kitchen. Although it has a television set, we've agreed that it will not be turned on until after dinner. Family members are welcome to gather in this room to read, talk, play board games or listen to music.

My habit is to sit down with a cup of tea and a book about 4 o'clock each afternoon. Although we have a television set and video games in the basement rec room, the children (ages eight to fourteen at the time of this writing) almost always choose to join me. Perhaps they crave peacefulness, as I do, after a busy day.

I firmly believe that the best way to create a cozy retreat for your family is to establish some clear ground rules for use of the room during specific times of the day. If children are squabbling over the remote control, the environment will be far from peaceful. Also, it's important to keep this room picked up and free of clutter. Nothing destroys a peaceful environment faster than piles of things that need attention.

Fluffy throw pillows, colorful quilts and soft throws encourage family members and guests to curl up in a chair, as does furniture upholstered in soft yet durable fabrics. Put on some soft music. Light candles for a soft glow or build a fire during the winter or on chilly fall days.

Our family enjoys the warmth of a fire so much that we decided to convert our fireplace to natural gas so we could have a blazing fire with a flip of the switch. Frankly, for a long time I balked at the idea of installing gas logs. Although modern gas logs look very natural, I was afraid I would miss the sounds and smell of a "real" fire. It only took one occasion in which the "ashes" glowed in the fireplace but didn't have to be scooped out to convince me to embrace this convenience.

Having a comfortable, cozy retreat has helped our family to slow down, even if it's only for an hour. Although we may be going separate ways after dinner, we've found time—and a place—to reconnect.

A Fragrant Offering

Then Mary took about a pint of pure nard, an expensive perfume; she poured it on Jesus' feet and wiped his feet with her hair. And the house was filled with the fragrance of the perfume. (John 12:3)

In my opinion, this love offering from Mary to Jesus is one of the most tender moments of worship recorded in the Bible. It's no mistake that she offered a fragrant oil to show her deep love for God. Throughout the history of Israel, God's people included incense as part of their sacrifices. Just as fragrance has been used to demonstrate devotion to God throughout the ages, I think using scent in our homes can also communicate love and devotion within the family.

Today, there are many choices for bringing a pleasant fragrance to your home, including scented candles, oil, potpourri—even pads that attach to your furnace filter to send a pleasant scent throughout the house whenever the fan kicks on. I checked my local grocery store and found almost an entire aisle of such products.

I'm not sure I buy into the aromatherapy movement which says certain scents are supposed to energize, relax or make you feel romantic. I tend to be the most energized or relaxed by scents that smell good to me. And, I would hope my husband feels romantic when he smells me—not a candle.

It's also been my experience that some of the best aromatherapy comes from the gift of God's provision to us. I love to bring in a bowl of lilacs and drink in their heady fragrance. The scent of a loaf of baking bread (in my breadmaker) almost always brings a smile to my husband's face when he walks in the door. The smell of cookies has the same effect on my children. And, personally, I think there is nothing better than the feel and scent of a freshly ironed pillowcase.

I want to encourage you to cherish the peace and joy that can be conveyed by a pleasant scent, and to offer a few minutes of your time to show your love and devotion to your family by delighting their senses with fragrance.

Treat Your Family like Company

He who refreshes others will himself be refreshed. (Proverbs 11:25)

I strive to make guests in our home feel special in many ways. I may prepare a special meal or dessert for dinner guests. For overnight guests, I try to make sure they are comfortable by putting a cozy quilt on the bed, laying out fluffy towels and perhaps putting a vase of fresh flowers in their bedroom. I want our guests to feel comfortable and refreshed while in our home.

One afternoon, as I was setting the table for a dinner party, my daughter came in with wide eyes and said, "Mom, this looks so beautiful! Your dinner club sure is lucky!" At that moment, I realized that while I routinely make special preparations for guests, I had rarely provided this kind of attention to my family. Keenly aware that my relationship with my husband and children are precious gifts from God, I made a decision to communicate just how special they are by treating them like company whenever I have the opportunity.

So, how do you treat your family like company and still drive carpool? Fortunately, this process requires more creativity than endurance. Here are a just few examples:

- Cut a few flowers from the garden and place a vase in your daughter's room.
- When making a special dessert for company, make two of them and tuck one in the freezer to serve at a family dinner.
- Instead of buying special coffee or tea only for guests, purchase it regularly so you can enjoy it with your husband.
- Light candles at dusk to provide a cozy glow.
- Set the table with your best dishes occasionally and eat by candlelight.
- Have dinner in the dining room using table linens.
- Bring your husband a breakfast tray that includes a fresh flower and the newspaper.

I occasionally carve out an hour or so in my day to make up a couple batches of cookie dough. I roll the dough into six-inch logs, wrap them tightly with plastic wrap and toss the dough in the freezer. To bake, just cut the log into half-inch slices, quarter each slice and place on a cookie sheet. This way, it just takes a few minutes to produce a batch of fresh, homemade cookies for an after-school treat. (Mrs. Cleaver would be so proud!)

I use the same principle to allow me to provide my special but time-consuming cinnamon rolls for my family before church on Sunday mornings. On a day when I have some extra time, I make a triple batch of sweet bread dough, allowing it to rise once. Then I assemble and slice the cinnamon rolls according to my recipe. Instead of allowing the rolls to rise, I place them on a greased cookie sheet and put them immediately into the freezer. When the rolls are frozen solid, I toss them into a self-sealing freezer bag.

The evening before I want to surprise my family with cinnamon rolls, I place the desired number of frozen rolls in a baking pan. I let them thaw and rise on the kitchen counter while we sleep. In the morning, I bake and frost the rolls as usual. What a treat it is for my family to wake up to the scent of freshly baked cinnamon rolls.

Serve one another in love. (Galatians 5:13)

Pass On Traditions

Tell it to your children,
and let your children tell it to their children,
and their children to the next generation. (Joel 1:3)

Traditions are extremely important to children. Experts say family rituals help to provide the sense of continuity and stability that is crucial to a child's development. I think it's important that we foster family traditions as well as pass them on to the next generation.

Family traditions don't have to be elaborate or complicated. Traditions can center around holidays and special occasions as well as everyday events. For example, your family might have a tradition of reading the Christmas story from Luke 2 on Christmas Eve, or reading a story and praying together before bedtime each evening. A tradition might be to go to a restaurant for brunch after church on Sunday mornings or to go home for a family dinner together. You might pick apples at a local orchard together every fall or visit the strawberry farm in June.

In Nebraska, fall means Big Red football. One of our favorite traditions is for each family member to prepare his or her favorite appetizer to share during the Nebraska football games. Liz usually makes guacamole, Anna wraps deli meat around pickles and cream cheese, and Freddy makes hot chili cheese dip. It makes no difference if the game is televised or on the radio, we still have our family football party!

We have another favorite tradition during the month of December. Each evening during the month we venture out for twenty or thirty minutes to look at Christmas lights and listen to Christmas carols on the car stereo. We have a map of the city and cross off neighborhoods as we visit them. The first person to spot a manger scene begins singing "Away in the Manger." We may seem a little goofy to onlookers, but we have a great time! My only fear is the possibility of my daughter insisting that we listen to the Christmas album of the latest teen heartthrob instead of Bing Crosby!

Recently my husband and children have begun a tradition of their own, a foosball game before bed each evening. Even though I think a nice, quiet bedtime story is probably a bit more conducive to settling down to sleep, they have so much fun that I wouldn't dare interfere.

In addition to fostering traditions, I think it's important that we make a conscious effort to pass them on. Teach your children how to prepare favorite family recipes. If you are a gardener, teach your children how to select, plant and tend the plants. When your children have their own homes, you can divide perennials and give the plants to them for their gardens. We have irises in our yard that originally came from my husband's great-grandmother—and wildflowers transplanted from the family farm.

One of the birthday traditions in our family is preparing a special chocolate raspberry cake. I used to purchase this cake from a local bakery. Then, several years ago, I experimented until I developed a pretty close approximation of the recipe that I could bake for a fraction of the cost of purchasing it. A couple of years ago Freddy asked me to teach him how to make this special dessert for a school project. I hadn't realized how well he had learned the recipe (which isn't written down anywhere) until he surprised me by preparing it for Mother's Day. Now Freddy is in the process of teaching his younger sister, Liz, how to make our "celebration" cake. Since Liz is the naturally organized member of our family, I'm sure she will write the recipe down and put it in a file for posterity.

So, whether simple or elaborate, let me encourage you to preserve the family traditions which make your family unique and draw you close to each other—and to God.

Spring Cleaning

I gave orders to purify the rooms. (Nehemiah 13:9)

I really hate to bring up this subject! It is definitely not a favorite topic of mine! Remember when June used to take off her pearls and tie the little dust cloth around her hair? This is what she was doing—spring cleaning.

No matter how orderly your life may be, you still have to take time to sweep away the cobwebs every so often. The good news is that spring cleaning is much easier to do in an orderly home. Not only will you have more time and energy because you're using your time more efficiently, but also spring cleaning is not so overwhelming when you've removed a lot of the clutter that was weighing you down.

The custom of spring cleaning began when homes were heated with wood or coal. It was necessary to clean one's home from top to bottom to remove the coat of grime that built up during the heating season. In those days, people washed walls, beat rugs, aired mattresses and pillows, washed windows and curtains, emptied drawers, closets and cabinets to clean their contents. Sounds fun, doesn't it?

Although I have never aired a mattress or beat a rug, there are some cleaning rituals I do my best to complete once a year, generally in the spring. It not only feels good to look through freshly washed windows and to know that you've vacuumed up anything that might have been growing under the sofa cushions, but I also find that I am more motivated to keep up with daily chores to keep our freshly spring-cleaned home looking nice.

Just what is "spring cleaning"? This term can mean different things to different people. One person may feel spring cleaning is washing and polishing every square inch of a home, while another may feel a good spring cleaning is simply vacuuming under the coffee table and sweeping out the garage. Both may be correct. It may include completing those home maintenance chores that you don't do on a regular basis but which still need to be done sometime. A good "sometime" is spring.

Here's my spring cleaning list:

- Clean windows, screens and window coverings throughout the house.
- Strip the beds and wash comforters, spreads, duvets, dust ruffles, etc.
- Purge and organize all closets, drawers and cabinets. (This should be a fairly easy task if you have followed the advice in chapters 2 and 3.)
- Clean walls, ceilings, woodwork and cabinets to remove grime, dust and cobwebs.
- Move all furniture and vacuum under and behind it.
- Thoroughly vacuum all upholstered pieces.
- Clean and dust books and bookshelves.
- Wax furniture.
- Clean and polish light fixtures.
- Shampoo carpeting.
- Purge and clean storage areas, including the garage.

Sound a bit overwhelming? It can be—if you look at spring cleaning as one monstrous event. The process is much more manageable if you break it up into smaller pieces. For example, take a Saturday afternoon to clean out the garage and another afternoon to wash windows. It also helps to involve your family. Not only will you finish more quickly, but family members will also gain an appreciation for the amount of work it takes to maintain a house. (And maybe after washing a few windows, they will be more careful about pressing their noses on the glass.)

I like to begin spring cleaning right after Christmas. I begin to get a touch of cabin fever in January and find the house looks a bit bleak without the holiday decorations. I've found that spring cleaning actually gives me an emotional lift. (Wonders never cease!)

I start by cleaning out the basement storage area since I need to find room for the Christmas decorations and assorted gifts. I then move on to purge closets, cabinets and drawers of all unneeded items (using the system outlined in chapter 2). Gradually I work my way around the house laundering, wiping, dusting and vacuuming. Next, I have the carpets shampooed and finish by washing the windows when the spring rains are over. It's a lot of work, but feels so good when complete. With spring cleaning out of the way, you'll be free to enjoy the warm, sunny days of the season.

Relax Your Standards

Now you have gone off because you longed to return to your father's house. (Genesis 31:30)

You probably think I am crazy to follow up encouragement to do spring cleaning with advice to relax your standards. Well, by now I'm sure you know that I am a little crazy, but I'm serious about this. It is so easy to allow our homes to become so perfectly decorated, clean or organized that they are miserable to live in. We need to maintain a balance in our lives to make sure our homes don't become idols.

One of the ways I have fought the urge toward perfectionism is to give in to my childish nature. My family (including my husband) loves it! For example, I am not adverse to allowing an occasional food fight (yes, that's right, food fight—as long as it's limited to the kitchen) to celebrate a birthday or other special occasion. I love water balloon fights in the backyard, and I sometimes even agree to stay up all night with the kids watching a movie marathon and eating junk food.

I'm convinced the memories of these "wild times" together are well worth mopping some water from the floor or occasionally scraping mashed potatoes off the wall. I don't want my family to feel like they are just residing in a house. I want them to feel they live in a home.

Now you probably have a better idea why spring cleaning is a necessity in our home.

> *Our mouths were filled with laughter,*
> *our tongues with songs of joy.* (Psalm 126:2)

Inspire Creativity and Spontaneity

> *My heart is stirred by a noble theme*
> *as I recite my verses for the king.* (45:1)

Believe it or not, I've found that the key to inspiring spontaneity and creativity is being prepared. Let me explain my thinking on this subject.

My children are much more likely to delve into a creative activity if the necessary materials are easily accessible. That's why we keep a closet in the rec room filled with all sorts of art and craft materials for their use. A tub filled with old clothing, hats, capes and costume jewelry has inspired many impromptu theatrical performances which became videotaped treasures. We've found that a bucket of side-walk chalk in the garage can lead to a masterpiece on the driveway, at least until the next rainstorm. I have also promised to never complain about a mess from these creative endeavors as long as the artists clean it up when they are finished.

Sometimes being spontaneous is much easier with a little planning. For example, it is much easier to have a spontaneous picnic in the park if the picnic basket is already equipped with basic supplies. In our basket, we keep paper plates, napkins, plastic utensils, paper cups, a tablecloth, powdered drink mix, a can of baked beans, a can opener, condiments, bug spray, a first-aid kit, matches and a small bag of "Match Light" charcoal briquettes which allows us to get a fire going by lighting the bag. All that's needed is a package of hot dogs and buns, a bag of chips and perhaps some fresh fruit. Remember to restock the picnic basket before it's put away so you can "be spontaneous" again soon.

Persevere

At this point, you may be thinking, *Wait! I don't have time to iron pillowcases, bring in fresh flowers or even think about spring cleaning! I haven't even bought my "clutter sorting tubs" yet!* Remember, all God asks is that you take one step at a time, but please don't put off taking that step.

Creating a haven for your family takes some extra time and a little flexibility, but it is well worth it. What a joy it is to see my daughter's eyes light up at the sight of fresh flowers in her room! Or to see my youngest curled up by the fire with a favorite book. Or to see my son grab a handful of cookies and join me on the back porch for a chat after school. Or to hear my husband come home after work and say, "Something sure smells good in here!"

Our youth pastor once passed on some very wise parenting advice. He said, "We can't isolate our kids from the world, but we can insulate them." I want to encourage you to trust God to help you provide all the insulation your family needs.

He guided them to their desired haven. (Psalm 107:30)

Going Deeper

1. How would you define "June's touch"? Why make the extra effort when you have many other things to do? See Colossians 3:23-24. Specifically, how can you incorporate some of "June's touch" in your home?

2. How can bringing nature into your home nurture spiritual growth? See Psalm 104, Matthew 6:28-30 and Romans 1:18-20.

3. Why is rest important to God? See Exodus 34:21 and Genesis 2:2-3. What can you do to make your home more restful?

4. What type of fragrance is pleasing to God? (See Genesis 8:20-21, 2 Corinthians 2:15 and Ephesians 5:1-2.)

5. In what ways can you use fragrance in your home to demonstrate your devotion to your family?

6. Spend some time sharing your family traditions. What makes these traditions special? What can you do to foster traditions in your family?

7. What can you do to treat your family "like company"? Why put out the effort? See Galatians 5:13 and Proverbs 11:25.

8. Why must we not isolate our children from the world? (See Matthew 9:9-13.) Why is it so important to provide insulation for our children? (See 1 John 5:19 and 1 Peter 5:8.) In what ways are you seeking to insulate your children?

CHAPTER NINE

Opening Your Heart and Home

Practice hospitality. (Romans 12:13)

Opening Your Heart and Home

Often, when I am reading a particularly convicting passage of Scripture, I find myself looking for a loophole. God's simple two-word command in Romans 12:13 to "practice hospitality" is an example.

The first time I came across this verse, I convinced myself that God probably meant something like, "It's a good idea to practice hospitality." Or, better yet, "Try to practice hospitality when you have some extra time and are in the mood to cook dinner and vacuum the rug." But as only the Holy Spirit can, God kept tugging on my heart until I had to admit He meant what He said—I was to practice hospitality. In other words: Just do it!

By now, you probably know enough about my personality to figure out that it is extremely difficult for me to "just do" anything. It's more of a process for me, unless the command is something like, "Eat another slice of cheesecake so it doesn't go to waste."

My first step in this process was to find out what God meant by "practice hospitality." The dictionary defines practice as "a customary action." The Amplified Bible further defines practice as "pursuing the practice of." In the King James Version, the verse reads "given to hospitality." Hospitality is defined by Webster's Dictionary as "the generous and cordial reception of guests." Now that I had a full grasp of the concept, I found a definite need for improvement in obedience. Why wasn't I practicing hospitality?

A Look Back

As a child, I was extremely hospitable. I loved to throw tea parties underneath the big pine tree on our front lawn. I would come outside with little teacups full of Kool-Aid and a platter full of store-bought chocolate chip cookies. I might even decide to whip up a treat in my Easy Bake Oven. (It still amazes me that I could bake cupcakes with a lightbulb!) I would invite all the little girls on the block to my teas, and we'd bring along our Raggedy Ann or Chatty Cathy dolls. Those tea parties were glorious!

As a teenager, too, it was easy to be hospitable. All I had to do was throw food on the table. It didn't matter if the food was still in the bag or can—there just had to be lots of it. When I was a young woman, friends felt free to stop by my apartment anytime for dinner or an impromptu get-together. In fact, my fiancé (now husband) thought I was a gourmet cook because I could heat crab legs in the micro-wave! Hospitality was a snap, and I loved to "practice" it.

As I took this little trip down memory lane, I began to realize that my slow drift away from practicing hospital-ity began shortly after I was married. In fact, it was within a few hours of the wedding ceremony when my brother-in-law offered a toast wishing us years of happiness and telling my husband how lucky he was to have me as his wife. At that moment, I realized that I was a wife and that the people offering all those toasts seemed to have pretty high expectations of me. After all, I had read Proverbs 31:11-12:

> *Her husband has full confidence in her*
> *and lacks nothing of value.*
> *She brings him good, not harm,*
> *all the days of her life.*

Great Expectations

I wasn't about to bring "harm" to my husband by serving appetizers from a bag, the main course from a box and dessert from the Easy Bake. In fact, shortly after we were married, I discovered that the wife of one of my husband's work associates made trays of homemade Christmas cookies for *all* of his clients. Talk about setting the bar high! Frankly, after marriage, hospitality seemed to be more about impressing than entertaining.

I worked to make sure our house was spotless from top to bottom, just in case someone wandered into the wrong room. Unfortunately, I picked up this habit due to an extremely embarrassing moment when a guest opened the door to our spare room. It was at that moment I realized that it was not the best place to store the laundry basket full of dirty dishes that I didn't have time to load in the dishwasher. I have now learned to stash them in the trunk of the car!

With those microwaved crab legs in mind, I explored another avenue to impress—culinary talent. I began to plan dinners I thought would showcase my cooking skills.

> *When pride comes, then comes disgrace.* (Proverbs 11:2)

I had a few close calls in this prideful pursuit—like almost setting my mother-in-law's hair on fire while trying to flame a dessert, or producing a gorgeous pie crust that required a chisel to cut. But the pièce de résistance was the night I tried to show off by whipping up a dish called "Chicken Margeaux" in front of our dinner guests. I picked up this idea from a friend who seemed to effortlessly prepare mouth-watering meals before our eyes. Now, he is a professional chef with his own restaurant, and I am still embarrassed about this incident.

I'm not sure what I did wrong, but the result was a sauce that strongly resembled sludge, and probably tasted like it. The more I tried to salvage it, the worse it became. As beads of sweat began to pop out on my forehead, my husband suggested serving salad and a double portion of dessert. Not exactly a Martha Stewart moment!

By setting unrealistic expectations for myself and my family, hospitality had become an extremely unpleasant experience. I would fret about the menu for weeks and spend days cleaning the house, sometimes even redecorating it. (I'll never forget deciding to paint the spare bedroom just forty-Five minutes before out-of-town guests were to arrive. I'm sure the paint fumes helped lull them to sleep.)

God calls us to "[o]ffer hospitality to one another without grumbling " (1 Peter 4:9). Always looking for that loophole, I thought, *What does God really mean by grumbling? Does He mean no grumbling in front of guests or . . . ?*

Lessons from a Monk

I know what you're thinking. By now I was probably so desperate for a loophole that I was checking out entering myself into a monastery. Close, but not quite. . . .

Brother Jerome has been the Guest Master at Mount Michael Monastery in Elkhorn, Nebraska for more than thirty years. He runs the Guest House on the property and offers lunches to visitors three days a week. A dear friend took me to lunch one day at this wonderful place, and my thoughts about the practice of hospitality have never been the same.

The lunches at Mount Michael are very special. I don't think it's because of the food, although it's tasty and beautifully presented. I'm also pretty sure it's not because of the decor, although Brother Jerome has done a beautiful job decorating the Guest House. There are restaurants closer to my home with good food and ambiance. However, there's something different about Mount Michael. I found myself returning time and time again.

Why? At first, it was hard to put my finger on what was so special about lunch at the Guest House. All I knew was that I felt completely comfortable and totally welcome. I also knew God had something to teach me about the practice of hospitality through Brother Jerome. So I mustered up the nerve to ask him to teach me how to "practice hospitality."

Convincing Brother Jerome to teach me was no easy task, for he saw nothing special about his practice of hospitality as Guest Master. I will always be grateful that he allowed God to pull him out of his comfort zone to share his wisdom.

Hospitality 101

The monks at Mount Michael belong to the Benedictine Order. This means they follow rules established by

Saint Benedict during the early years of the church. Saint Benedict's Rule 51 states: "All guests should be received as Christ." What a wonderful picture of the practice of hospitality! Brother Jerome strongly feels all humans should be treated with the utmost dignity and respect since all are created in God's image (Genesis 1:27).

It was also very interesting and enlightening to learn that Brother Jerome considers hospitality a form of worship. He believes when we practice hospitality well and with grace, it is a powerful tribute to God.

> So whether you eat or drink or whatever you do, do it
> all for the glory of God. (1 Corinthians 10:31)

Brother Jerome led me through several passages in Scripture that deal with hospitality. In Luke 14:12-14, Jesus warns us not only to entertain relatives and those who can afford to pay us back, but also to offer hospitality to those who may not be able to return the favor such as "the poor, the crippled, the lame, the blind." Jesus promises that our hospitality "will be repaid at the resurrection of the righteous."

These verses helped me to understand why lunch at the Guest House is free of charge to all who come. The monastery is willing to accept a donation for the Lord's work, but a guest is never presented a bill. Guests are also free to stroll through the beautiful gardens. There is even a small house adjacent to the main building that is available for a spiritual retreat, or just a day of rest.

> Do not forget to entertain strangers, for by so doing some
> people have entertained angels without knowing it.
> (Hebrews 13:2)

Brother Jerome firmly believes that everything we do leaves fingerprints on those we touch. I know that his touch pointed me to God and His gracious acceptance of me as an heir. Brother Jerome prompted me to think about what kind of fingerprints I wanted to leave on those I touched.

Principles of Hospitality

Through observation and the gentle tutoring of Brother Jerome, I have embraced six principles to guide me as I obey the Lord by practicing hospitality. These principles helped me put the practice of hospitality in the proper perspective and gave me the courage once again to open my home not for my glory, but for His. I hope these principles serve as a guide and encouragement to you also.

Share Your Presence

People often try to limit hospitality to providing food or a place to sleep. I challenge you to stop and think for a moment. Why do you accept an invitation to someone's home? Is it only for a place to sleep or to avoid cooking for an evening? I doubt it. Our guests crave our company, our presence. Our gift to them is our attention both emotionally and physically.

What does this mean practically? It means that you need to do some planning to be truly available emotionally and physically to your guests. The first step is the menu. When we are having company for a meal, I almost always select dishes that can be assembled several hours ahead of time and cooked in the oven. In the summer, when it's too hot for the oven, I plan a menu that can be cooked on the grill.

173

It's also fun to plan a dinner that guests can "create" to-gether—like a giant submarine sandwich, super burritos or individual pizzas.

Our family also enjoys a trip back to the days of the "Bradys" when every home had an avocado or burnt orange fondue pot. Our kids call these parties "Fondue Magic!" We usually serve a simple cheese fondue with bread cubes as an appetizer. Then we set an electric fondue pot with hot oil or broth in the middle of the dining room table and allow guests to select, cook and eat small pieces of meat and vegetables while we talk. We pass a variety of store-bought sauces (BBQ, sweet and sour, horseradish, seafood etc.) for dipping. Chocolate fondue with cake and fruit for dipping follows for dessert. All this dipping encourages hours of great conversation.

In addition to being present physically, it's important to be there emotionally for your guests. You will find that planning ahead frees your mind. For a large dinner, I always put together a timetable and make good use of my oven timer to remind me to check on things. This allows me to concentrate on my guests, instead of the stove.

Don't Allow Preparations to Hamper God's Purpose

The story of Jesus' visit to the house of His good friends, Mary and Martha (Luke 10:38-42), is a wonderful lesson on the practice of hospitality. Martha was rushing around preparing dinner while Mary sat at Jesus's feet. Martha spies her sister "goldbricking" and complains to Jesus, "Lord, don't you care that my sister has left me to do all the work by myself? Tell her to help me!" Jesus replies, "Martha, Martha, . . . you are worried and upset about many things. . . . Mary has chosen what is better and it will not be taken from her" (10:41-42). I bet that wasn't the answer Martha was expecting!

I think we can all see ourselves in Martha's shoes at one time or another. It's easy to get into such a frenzy with preparations that we miss God's purpose for opening up our home to others. Don't let this happen to you.

I have developed a habit to remind me to behave more like Mary and leave my Martha tendencies in the kitchen with my apron. During appetizers, I place the food on the coffee table, sit on the floor, spread cheese on crackers (or whatever) and pass the hors d'oeuvres directly to our guests.

I have learned from experience that creating a frenzy in preparation for guests can have a profoundly negative impact on your family. In the past, when we were expecting company, I promptly took on the role of drill sergeant. "Pick up this! Dust this! Polish this! Scrub this! Scrub this again!" The kids would dread having company and would do anything to get out of the house. Yet they too are also accountable to obey God's command of practicing hospitality. Sadly, before they even had a chance to whip up a cake in their Easy Bake Oven, I was teaching them that hospitality is a practice to be avoided at all costs.

> But if anyone causes one of these little ones who believe
> in me to sin, it would be better for him to have a large
> millstone hung around his neck and to be drowned in
> the depths of the sea. (Matthew 18:6)

If you find yourself in the role of drill sergeant when expecting company, my advice is to relax, turn the lights down low to hide the dust and lose the whistle before you find a millstone in its place.

Don't Let Your Service Become Self-Serving

If you find yourself in a frenzy about preparations for guests, I strongly suggest examining your motives for insisting on a spotless house or preparing a six-course meal. When I looked at my own motives, it was not a pretty picture. The focal point, I discovered, was pride. God does not command us to practice hospitality so we look good to others. We should use our homes to bring glory to God, not to ourselves. An elaborate meal may even intimidate some guests. The more hospitable option may be a simple pot of soup and loaf of warm bread.

The same principle applies to a spotless house. An orderly home is peaceful, but we can easily go overboard and make our home an obstacle to the comfort of guests. I remember being extremely nervous at an acquaintance's home trying to balance my coffee and dessert and sitting on a white silk sofa that rested on spotless white carpeting. Ask God to help you find the balance to make your home comfortable and welcoming for guests.

My mother had a very wise saying, "My house is clean enough to be healthy and dirty enough to be happy." Amen!

Everything We Do Has Eternal Significance

It's important to remember that God generally accomplishes the extraordinary through the ordinary. Take the time to listen to the promptings of the Holy Spirit to reach out to a friend or neighbor with a cup of tea. Or invite that new family in your church to Sunday dinner after worship. You might even feel led to host a Christmas outreach for the neighbors with whom you only communicate by waving from the car window as you buzz down the street.

Opportunities for hospitality can be terrific blessings to both you and your guests—but the key is to be prepared. You might tuck away some muffins in your freezer to serve with a cup of tea or coffee. Keep a large casserole (like lasagna) in the freezer for spur-of-the-moment guests. Have the ingredients on hand to put together a simple tray of snacks. But most importantly, listen to the whisper of the Holy Spirit calling you to reach out.

> *Whatever your hand finds to do, do it with all your might.* (Ecclesiastes 9:10)

Let God Feed You Before You Try to Feed Others

I've said this over and over, but it is the central truth of this book. Before reaching out to others, we must first seek His kingdom and His righteousness. (See Matthew 6:33.) Let the Lord grow in you through reading His Word, meditating upon it and coming to Him in prayer each day. Ask Him to alert you to the opportunities that He has for you to practice hospitality. Pray for flexibility and the desire to reach out to others. Ask Him to help you grow in love and compassion. As you let God teach you, nurture your spirit and fill you with His Holy Spirit, you can't help but reflect His light to others.

When I began to obey God by practicing hospitality in His way, He began to shower me with blessing after blessing. He has restored the days of my youth as I once again love to entertain. One of these days, I might even set up a little tea party under the pine tree in our backyard. . . .

Through the practice of hospitality, I have been able to develop lifelong friendships and a system of support and encouragement. I have also begun to understand the reason behind God's command to practice hospitality. Christian hospitality can be a powerful tool for furthering His kingdom.

Many people have commented that my home is a warm and welcoming place, but the greatest compliment came from a three-year-old child whose mother was a nonbeliever at the time. After looking at her daughter asleep on my sofa, she exclaimed, "Look at how peacefully she's sleeping! She has never felt comfortable enough to fall asleep anywhere else except at home."

So, my greatest hope when opening the door to my home is not that guests will see a spotless house, beautifully decorated, or smell the aroma of a fabulous meal in the oven, or notice well-scrubbed children with impeccable manners.

My prayer is that as I open the door to my home, my guests will see in my eyes and relaxed smile the tender, perfect, beautiful love of Christ.

Will you let Him shine through you?

> *For you were once darkness, but now you are light in the Lord. Live as children of light.* (Ephesians 5:8)

Going Deeper

1. Do you think people today are more or less hospitable? Share the reason for your answer.

2. What are some of the specific blessings you have received from offering hospitality to others? What about blessings you have received as the recipient of hospitality?

3. Try to recall a time when you thoroughly enjoyed the hospitality of another. What made the occasion so special?

4. Read Romans 12:13. Why do you think God gives this command?

5. In the Greek, Romans 12:13 could be more closely translated as "pursue hospitality." In what ways could you actively pursue opportunities to offer hospitality to other people?

6. Read Luke 14:12-14. What is Jesus instructing us to do in this passage? How can you practically put this command into practice?

7. Read Genesis 18:1-8. Describe the hospitality offered by Abraham. What impresses you about the way Abraham received the three strangers? What can you learn from his example?

8. Read Luke 10:38-42 and First Peter 4:9. What do you learn from these passages? Do you see yourself more in the role of Mary or Martha? What do you need to do to make the offer of hospitality a pleasant experience for you and your family?

9. Spend some time sharing your ideas for offering hospitality with the group.

CHAPTER TEN

From
My
Heart to
Yours

Likewise, teach the older women to be reverent in the way they live, not to be slanderers or addicted to much wine, but to teach what is good. Then they can train the younger women to love their husbands and children, to be self-controlled and pure, to be busy at home, to be kind, and to be subject to their husbands, so that no one will malign the word of God. (Titus 2:3-5)

From My Heart to Yours

Dear Reader, I am sitting in my chair with a cup of tea and I'm thinking about you, wondering who you are, what struggles you are facing and how you are feeling as you reach the last chapter of this book. Are you encouraged or discouraged?

A lump forms in my throat as I remember my struggles as a young wife and mother. I know the feeling of being overwhelmed by the management of my home, feeling like I was on an out-of-control roller coaster headed right into the mountain of dirty laundry at the bottom of the stairs. I've felt the pang of guilt after snapping at my husband or children because of the chaos around me. I've felt the frustration of wasted time and energy because I couldn't find something I needed.

As I remember, I long to give each one of you a hug of encouragement and whisper, "Keep going! It's worth it!" But I know from personal experience that my hugs or words are not what you really need. Whether you realize it or not, your soul is crying out to your Creator for the help and peace that only He can give. And so, from my heart to yours, I want to share some of His words.

Consider these "spiritual hugs" with the power to comfort, encourage and strengthen you.

Draw Near

Draw near to God and He will draw near to you.
(James 4:8, NASB)

As I have said throughout the book, it's not the method or system that will transform your home into a haven for your family. It's God who will make the difference by teaching you His ways. We need to turn our lives, as well as our homes, over to Him.

There was a time in my life when I thought that if I tried hard enough and was a good enough person, I would have a place in heaven. But, as I searched the Bible, I found that my trust in good works was a lie. I thank God every day for showing me the truth.

The Bible says all people have sinned and fallen short of God's standards (Romans 3:23) and the penalty for even one sin is death and eternal separation from God (6:23). To God, sin is sin, whether it's murder, gossip . . . or snapping at our children. He is just and holy, and He abhors all forms of sin.

But God loves us and has a plan for His people (Jeremiah 29:11-13). He doesn't choose to have us wallow in our sin with no hope.

> *"For I know the plans I have for you," declares the LORD, "plans to prosper you and not to harm you, plans to give you hope and a future." (29:11)*

God loves us so much that He sent His only Son, Jesus, to live the perfect life we can't. Then, Jesus took the punishment for the sin of the world by dying on the cross.

For God so loved the world that he gave his one and only Son, that whoever believes in him shall not perish but have eternal life. (John 3:16)

There is nothing we can do to save ourselves. We can never be good enough. We just need to believe, to trust Jesus for our salvation.

I'll never forget the day I understood this message of salvation. For the first time, God's plan made sense to me. I was overwhelmed with grief for my sin while at the same time amazed and full of deep gratitude for the gift of salvation God was holding out to me. I got down on my knees, admitted my sin to God and accepted His gift of forgiveness. From that day forward, I was assured of a place in heaven.

Now, I am going to ask you the most important question of your life. Do you have this assurance of forgiveness and salvation? If not, don't wait another minute. Go to God in prayer, admit your sin, ask for forgiveness and accept His work on the cross as payment for your sin. That's all you need to do. God will do the rest.

If you confess with your mouth, "Jesus is Lord," and believe in your heart that God raised him from the dead, you will be saved. (Romans 10:9)

Jesus Christ came to earth and died in our place so that we could have life and live it abundantly. Only by placing our faith in Him alone can we "draw near" as a true child of God.

The LORD is good, . . . He cares for those who trust in him. (Nahum 1:7)

Pump Some Iron

> The strain of life is what builds strength. If there is
> no strain, there is no strength.
>
> —Oswald Chambers
> *My Utmost for His Highest*, August 2

There's a song I often hear on the Christian radio station that says "Life is hard, but God is good." And, you know, the more I think about it, I believe God is good *because* life is hard. If life were easy, few would seek Him. As a result, we would miss out on the great blessings He has for those He calls His own, not to mention the promise of eternal life. I truly believe that God often uses trials to draw us to Him because He knows better than anyone how empty we are without Him.

> *We know that suffering produces perseverance; perseverance, character; and character, hope. And hope does not disappoint us.* (Romans 5:3-5)

Our hope is Jesus Christ, and He promises never to disappoint us. You can be sure God Almighty will give you the strength you need when you need it most.

> *The LORD is my strength and my song;*
> *he has become my salvation.* (Psalm 118:14)

Walk with God

> *Trust in the LORD with all your heart*
> *and lean not on your own understanding;*
> *in all your ways acknowledge him,*
> *and he will make your paths straight.*
> (Proverbs 3:5-6)

About the only straight path I can make on my own is to the refrigerator. But when I walk with God, trusting Him to guide me using His Word as "a lamp unto my feet" (Psalm 119:105), it is amazing where He takes me. I just need to be willing to go—and to hold tightly to His hand.

> *I am the vine; you are the branches. If a man remains in me and I in him, he will bear much fruit; apart from me you can do nothing.* (John 15:5)

Don't loosen your grip on the vine!

Say Yes!

> *Then I heard the voice of the Lord saying, "Whom shall I send? And who will go for us?"*
> *And I said, "Here am I. Send me!"* (Isaiah 6:8)

When your answer to God's call is "Here am I. Send me!" you can be certain He will use you. He also won't call you to anything that He doesn't also provide the strength, creativity and/or patience to accomplish.

It's important to resist the temptation to compare yourself with others as you ponder His call. God created you perfectly suited for His purposes. He does not expect you to be anyone or anything except who He created you to be. There are things that you do better than others and things that others do better than you. We are all valuable parts of the body of Christ. We just need to do our part.

> *Just as each of us has one body with many members, and these members do not all have the same function, so in Christ we who are many form one body, and each member belongs to all the others.* (Romans 12:4-5)

Persevere

Whatever you do, do it all for the glory of God. (1 Co-rinthians 10:31)

We need to hold fast to the truth that the work we do in our homes has eternal significance. It will leave a lasting imprint on future generations. The world may try repeatedly to trivialize it. Satan may do all he can to discourage you and sap your strength. But remember, the peace that comes from a well-run home is in stark contrast to the chaos of our society. Your family needs a haven from the pressures of the world, and they need a powerful example of a woman who is dependent on the Lord for all things.

Your dependence on God will not only impact your family, but it will also have a profound impact on the world around you. The results of submitting your life and home to God's control will make such a difference that people will be attracted as if to an irresistible fragrance.

The Bible tells us the harvest is ripe. People are hungry for the spiritual truth found only at the cross of Jesus Christ. You know the One their souls are longing for—and it's definitely not Alice. It's Jesus. Won't you make a commitment today to let the light of Christ shine through you and your home as a beacon to the lost?

> *[Her] delight is in the law of the LORD,*
>   *and on his law [she] meditates day and night.*
> *[She] is like a tree planted by streams of water,*
>   *which yields its fruit in season*
> *and whose leaf does not wither.*
>   *Whatever [she] does prospers. . . .*
> *For the LORD watches over the way of the righteous.*
>   (Psalm 1:2-3, 6)

Going Deeper

1. What is standing in the way of making your home a haven for your family and others?
2. Read James 4:8. What must we—you and I—do to truly draw near to God? Have you drawn near to Him by trusting Him alone for your salvation? If you are not sure that if you died tonight you would be with God in heaven, turn to pages 184-185 and read the section and drawing near to God.
3. Read Romans 5:3-5. Have you experienced this promise as you make your home a ministry? In what way?
4. Read Romans 12:4-6. How are you employing your God-given gifts for the benefit of the body of Christ?
5. Read First Corinthians 10:31. How can ministry in the home glorify God?
6. What changes have you made in your life as a result of this study? What changes do you need to make? Read Matthew 6:33 and John 15:5. Stand on these promises!

A Few of
My
Favorite
Recipes

He has given food and provision to those who reverently and worshipfully fear Him. (Psalm 111:5, AMP)

A Few of My Favorite Recipes

Fabulous Marinade

1 large clove garlic, crushed
1/2 cup oil
1/4 cup soy sauce
1 tablespoon Worcestershire sauce
1/4 cup wine vinegar
1/8 cup lemon juice
1 tablespoon Dijon mustard
1/2 teaspoon salt
1/2 teaspoon pepper
1 tablespoon parsley

Whisk together and follow the directions below for the meat(s) you have selected. This versatile marinade can be used with chicken, fish, pork, beef and ground meat.

CHICKEN: Place 1/2 cup of marinade in freezer bag. Add frozen chicken breasts. Seal. To serve: thaw and grill.

PORK: Place 1/2 cup of marinade in freezer bag. Add frozen cubed pork or boneless pork chops. Seal. To serve: thaw and thread cubes on skewers with mixture of fresh vegetables (mushrooms, onions, peppers). Grill. Baste with marinade during the first half of the cooking time.

FISH: Place 1/2 cup of marinade in a freezer bag. Freeze fish filets in separate freezer bag. Marinate 10-30 minutes before grilling or broiling. Baste with marinade while cooking until fish flakes.

BEEF: Place 1/2 cup marinade in freezer bag. Add sirloin or London broil. Seal. To serve: thaw and grill to desired doneness.

GROUND MEAT: Add 1/4 cup marinade to lean hamburger or other ground meat. Shape into patties and place in freezer bag. Place buns in a separate freezer bag and package together in a two-gallon bag. To serve: thaw and grill or broil. Serve on buns.

Basic Meat Mixture

1 egg, beaten, or egg substitute
3/4 cup soft bread crumbs
1/4 cup chopped onion
1 1/2 pounds very lean ground beef
1/2 cup shredded carrots
1/2 teaspoon salt
1/4 teaspoon pepper

Mix all ingredients together. From this mixture, you can make one of the following dishes:

Savory Meatloaf

Add to above basic meat mixture:
1/4 cup milk
1 teaspoon dried (or 1 tablespoon fresh) sage leaves
2 tablespoons catsup

Place in freezer bag, flatten. Seal. To serve: thaw meat mixture and shape into loaf or ring. Place in pan and bake at 350° until no longer pink in the center, about 40-45 minutes.

Italian Meatballs

Add to the above basic meat mixture:
2 cups favorite meatless spaghetti sauce
1/4 cup milk
2 teaspoon fennel seed
1 large clove garlic, crushed

Shape into meatballs. Bake meatballs on broiler pan at 375° until cooked through. Cool. Transfer to one-gallon freezer bag. Add spaghetti sauce and freeze.

To make Italian Meatball Sandwiches, freeze meatballs in bag with spaghetti sauce. Place in separate bags 1 cup mozzarella cheese and

4-6 hard rolls. Place all bags in one two-gallon bag to keep together.

To serve: thaw. Heat meatballs in sauce until heated through. Split hard rolls, top with meatballs and sauce and sprinkle with mozzarella cheese.

The above meatball mixture can also be shaped into a loaf for Italian Meatloaf or patties for pizza burgers.

International Stew

This stew offers a culinary world tour when you add just a few ingredients to the basic recipe!

Starter Stew

4-5 pounds boneless stew meat (lean)
2 tablespoons minced garlic
2-3 cans beef broth (whatever fits in your pot)
3 cups chopped onions

Put all ingredients in crockpot. Cook on low overnight (10-12 hours) or high 5-6 hours. Divide into 4 portions in one-gallon freezer bags. This mixture can be seasoned to make the following meals:

Beef Bordeaux

Place in freezer bag:
3-4 cups starter stew
1 package frozen baby carrots
1 cup sliced mushrooms
1/2 teaspoon each salt, pepper, thyme
1 cup beef broth
1 cup unsweetened red grape juice
1 package frozen cooked egg noodles (freeze separately)

195

To serve: thaw stew and heat. Remove 1/2 cup liquid and stir in 2 tablespoons flour. Return to stew. Heat until bubbling. Adjust seasonings. Serve over cooked noodles. Garnish with chopped parsley.

Osso Bucco

Place in freezer bag:
 3-4 cups starter stew
 1 16-ounce package frozen baby carrots
 1 16-ounce can chopped tomatoes (or chopped fresh)
 1/4 teaspoon each: basil, thyme
 1 cup unsweetened white grape juice
 1 package risotto (store in pantry)

To serve: thaw stew and heat. Remove 1/2 cup liquid and stir in 2 tablespoons flour. Return to stew. Heat until bubbling. Adjust seasonings. Serve over risotto. Garnish with chopped parsley.

Middle Eastern

Place in freezer bag:
 3-4 cups starter stew
 1 8-ounce can tomato sauce
 1/2 cup water
 1/3 teaspoon each: ginger, cinnamon, nutmeg
 1 teaspoon each cumin, oregano
 2 cups frozen carrots
 1 bunch fresh spinach
 1 package couscous (store in pantry)
 1/2 cup raisins

To serve: thaw stew and heat. Remove 1/2 cup liquid and stir in 2 tablespoons flour. Return to stew. Heat until bubbling. Serve over cooked couscous mixed with raisins. Garnish with chopped cilantro, if desired.

Southwestern

Place in freezer bag:

> 3-4 cups starter stew
> 1 16-ounce package frozen corn
> 1 small bunch chopped cilantro
> 2 teaspoons cumin
> 1/4 teaspoon red pepper
> 2 tablespoons sugar
> salt and pepper to taste
> 2 16-ounce cans Mexican style tomatoes
> 1 15-ounce can red kidney beans (drained)
> 1 cup dry rice (store in pantry)

To serve: thaw stew and heat. Remove 1/2 cup liquid and stir in 2 tablespoons flour. Return to stew. Heat until bubbling. Serve over cooked rice. Garnish with chopped cilantro, if desired.

Oriental

Place in freezer bag:

> 3-4 cups starter stew
> 1 16-ounce package frozen stir-fry vegetables
> 1 bunch chopped green onions
> 1 teaspoon each: grated orange peel, ginger
> 1/2 cup stir-fry sauce
> 1 cup dry rice (store in pantry)

To serve: thaw and heat. Remove 1/2 cup liquid and stir in 2 tablespoons flour. Return to stew. Heat until bubbling. Serve over cooked rice. Garnish with sliced scallions, if desired.

Sample Game Plan

The recipes indicated with a star are included on pages 193-197. All recipes included in the Sample Game Plan can be found in my cookbook *The Occasional Cook*.

The day before cooking day:

- Chop 7 pounds onions
- Chop 3 green peppers
- Slice 2 bunches green onions
- Slice 2 cups mushrooms
- Shred 1 pound carrots
- Process 7 cups bread crumbs
- Assemble basic stew, simmer in crockpots (divide in two)
- Cool basic stew in refrigerator
- Assemble marinara sauce, simmer in crockpot (1x)
- Assemble chili and simmer (1x)
- Package rolls, rice, chips and cheese
- Cool marinara
- Cool chili

Cooking day . . .

- Start water to boil pasta (1x)
- ★ Assemble basic meat mixture (5x)
- ★ Assemble mixture for Italian Meatballs (3x)
- Shape meatballs, bake
- ★ Assemble Savory Meatloaf, package (1x)

- Assemble Baked Pasta, package (1x)
- Assemble Italian Chicken, package (1x)
★ Package meatballs for Italian Hoagies (1x)
- Package Spaghetti with Meatballs (2x)
★ Assemble Southwestern Stew (2x), package
★ Assemble Beef Bordeaux (2x), package
★ Assemble Oriental Stew (2x), package
- Make salsa (4x), package
- Assemble Tom's Tacos (2x), package
- Assemble Taco Salad (1x), package
- Assemble Southwestern Bakers (1x), package
★ Make Savory Marinade (3x)
- Package Marinated Chicken (2x)
★ Package Savory Burgers (1x)

Supplemental
Resources

Make plans by seeking advice.
(Proverbs 20:18)

Supplemental Resources

Devotional Guides

Although I feel strongly that the Holy Bible is the primary path to the heart of God, I have found devotional guides to be helpful and thought provoking as I made use of them during my quiet time. The best of these guides rely heavily on the Word of God.

Here are my favorites:

1. International Bible Society. *The One Year Bible*. Wheaton, Illinois: Tyndale House Publishers, Inc., 1986. (The entire Bible is arranged in 365 daily readings with passages from both the Old and New Testaments as well as a Psalm and Proverb.)
2. Boa, Kenneth. *Face to Face: Praying the Scriptures for Intimate Worship*. Grand Rapids, Michigan: Zondervan Publishing House, 1997. (Personalized adaptations of Scripture which turn Bible passages into prayers.)
3. Chambers, Oswald. *My Utmost for His Highest*, updated edition in today's language. Edited by James Reimann. Grand Rapids, Michigan: Discovery House Publishers, 1992. (Classic devotionals which powerfully apply the truth of God's Word to daily living. This updated version is very readable.)
4. Roberts, Lee. *Praying God's Will for My Husband*. Nashville, Tennessee: Thomas Nelson Publishers, 1993. (Book of prayers drawn from God's Word and applied to the needs of husbands.)
5. Osbeck, Kenneth W. *101 Hymn Stories*. Grand Rapids, Michigan: Kregel Publications, 1982. (Collection of uplifting and informative stories behind many favorite hymns.)

6. Munger, Robert Boyd. *My Heart—Christ's Home.* Downers Grove, Illinois: InterVarsity Press, 1986. (Small booklet vividly illustrating total surrender to Christ.)
7. Foster, Marilynne E., ed. *Tozer on the Holy Spirit.* Camp Hill, Pennsylvania: Christian Publications, Inc., 2000. (366-day devotional of pithy, incisive and refreshing quotes taken from the many works of classic author A.W. Tozer.)

Prayer Rock

I use my prayer rock to remind me to set a daily appointment with God. I place the rock on my pillow when making the bed in the morning. When I pull back the covers before retiring, I am reminded to ask God to help me rise in time for my morning quiet time. He is very faithful!

Here's how you can make your own prayer rock. You will need:

- one smooth, medium-sized rock
- one square of fabric about six inches square
- six inches of ribbon
- a rubber band

Directions:
Lay the rock in the center of the fabric. Pull the corners to meet at the top and gather the fabric around the rock. Wind the rubber band around the neck of the fabric. Tie a bow with the ribbon over the rubber band.

Organizational Helps by Mail Order

Many organizational gadgets and supplies can now be found in discount, hardware or home specialty stores, but mail-order companies can also be wonderful sources for many of these items. Contact the company directly for a free catalog.

Here are my favorites:

- "Solutions"—1-800-342-9988
- "Lillian Vernon Catalog"—1-800-285-5555
- "Plow and Hearth"—1-800-627-1712
- "Martha by Mail"—1-800-950-7130
- "Williams-Sonoma Catalog"—1-800-541-2233
- "L.L. Bean Home"—1-800-221-4221

Many of these vendors may also have web sites which provide online shopping. Call them directly for their Internet address or search the web by typing in a keyword.

You may request information regarding additional resources as well as Cyndy's workshops and seminars by writing to:

Cyndy Salzmann
c/o Family Haven Ministries
15905 Jones Circle
Omaha, Nebraska 68118

or visit Cyndy's Web site at:
www.familyhavenministries.com